PRAYERS OF THE FAITHFUL

PRAYERS OF THE FAITHFUL

Cycles A, B, C

A PUEBLO BOOK

The Liturgical Press   Collegeville, Minnesota

Nihil Obstat:

Joseph P. Penna, J.C.D.
Censor Librorum

Imprimatur:

✠ James P. Mahoney, D.D.
Vicar General,
Archdiocese of New York

Design: Frank Kacmarcik, Obl.S.B.

These prayers were previously published in *Liturgical Prayer Magazine*. The authorship of each prayer was often not specified, so for the purpose of acknowledgment we list below many who contributed to this journal.

Thomas Wahl, O.S.B.; Rev. Robert Morhous, Peter Scagnelli, Rev. Robert Imbelli, Sr. Regina Bechtle, Sr. Marjorie Moffatt, Rev. Herbert F. Brokering, Rev. James F. Moon, Rev. Thomas B. Woodward, Linda Schmid, Anthony P. Scully, Sharlene Shoemaker, Barbara Wolf, Robert Auletta, James F. Miffit, Sr. Joanne Evans, Rev. Martin T. Geraghty, Sr. Bonnie Motto, Martha Brown, Sr. Joyce Hibbert, Marguerite M. Iott, Jack Lindeman, Rev. Paul J. LeBlanc, Sr. Rose Ann Quigley, Sr. Dorothy Whelan, Carol DeChristopher, Rev. Henry Fehren, Sr. Margaret Kelleher, Charles Liggio, Sr. Rose Agnes MacCanley, Kathleen Dugan, Nathan Mitchell, O.S.B.; Rev. Robert W. Hovda, Anne Jones, Rita Ann Moceri, Patricia Pettis, Mary Spielman, Sr. Nancy Swift, Lynne Wehrman, Sam Bradley, Priscilla Piche, William Skudlarek, O.S.B.; Susan Haugland, Paul Jones, Sally Wilson, James Dolan, John McGuigan, Rev. Peter Fink, James Sullivan, Rev. Gerald Siegler.

Printed in the United States of America.

ISBN 0-8146-6029-0

TABLE OF CONTENTS

SOLEMNITIES AND FEASTS

RITUAL

PREFACE

The Prayer of the Faithful, or general intercessions, restored to the eucharistic liturgy in the liturgical reforms following Vatican Council II has by now become common practice. In this prayer "the people exercise their priestly function by praying for all mankind" (General Instruction on the Roman Missal, no. 45).

According to the sacramentary, the sequence of intentions is usually as follows: a) for the needs of the Church, b) for public authorities and the salvation of the world, c) for those oppressed by any need, and d) for the local community. The list of intentions may be more closely concerned with special occasions such as confirmation, marriages, funerals, etc. Further, "In the Prayer of the Faithful, besides the petitions for the Church, the world and the needy, it is good to add some special intentions for the local community . . . .

"Priests should be led to prepare their celebration, taking into consideration the circumstances and spiritual needs of the faithful" (Third Instruction on the Correct Implementation of the Constitution on the Sacred Liturgy, no. 3g).

Thus, there is a certain flexibility as to the subject of the various intentions, their number and sequence.

After the profession of faith the priest directs the prayer by giving a brief introduction inviting the people to pray. The petitions are then announced by the deacon, cantor or other person, and the congregation responds either by a common response after each petition or by silent prayer. The common response is almost universal practice now. The priest then says a concluding prayer, always addressed to God the Father.

The introduction is addressed to the people, not to God, and it usually suggests the broad theme of the prayers to follow. This preliminary invitation, according to the Newsletter of the Bishops Committee on the Liturgy, relates the general intercessions to the mystery being celebrated, the feast or saint of the day, or some particular theme or lesson from the homily or the readings. It calls forth a response from the people.

On each particular occasion the response should be the same for all the petitions, though it may differ from one celebration to the next. The priest does not prefix the usual "Let us pray" to the concluding prayer.

We present this volume of general intercessions only as a resource book for expressing the needs of the faithful. All ritual, to be effective and to be one in which the participants can be somewhat comfortable, must have elements which are stable and unchanging. Yet the form and content must not be a canned production, but must have variety and life and should be a stimulant to prayer for the immediate group involved.

It is important, as it is in all of liturgy, that the meaning of the petitions be clear to the people. People cannot give interior assent (though they often give mere verbal consent and thus true prayer is lost) when the petitions are too complex for immediate understanding. Brevity is not only the soul of wit; it is essential for clarity in a series of petitions.

Formulating petitions is not an easy task. They should be fresh, clear, varied, and of immediate concern, yet not overly dramatic, or, what is worse, coy, cute or obviously clever. As in all of liturgy, which is public prayer of all the assembly, the Prayer of the Faithful must have a sense of classic restraint.

Petitions should not be didactic, and should not be used as a sledge-hammer to force upon the people a series of merely personal petitions. The prayers should not be used to manipulate the faithful.

The number of petitions may vary, but too long a list makes the prayers lose their immediacy and induces boredom. In this volume we have suggested five for each celebration, and left space for other petitions, of more immediate concern to the local congregation, to be written in. Also, there can be a time of silence for private intentions.

The petitions in this book, since they attempt to express the needs and concerns of present-day congregations, have been composed by various people, young and old, clerical, religious and lay. Even so, as one priest has pointed out, "prayer is in the praying and not in the composition.

Henry Fehren

A CYCLE
FIRST SUNDAY OF ADVENT

Celebrant:
In Advent we prepare for a temporal and an eternal feast. We
look forward to a birth, the birth of Christ, and we anticipate the
birth of our life in heaven and the completion of the kingdom.

Leader:
That we be awake when the Lord comes, and be awake to the
many ways in which He comes to us , let us pray to the Lord.

2.
That our hearts be prepared for the kingdom of God within
ourselves and for the fullness of the kingdom at Christ's
second coming, let us pray to the Lord.

3.
That Advent be a time of true repentance lest with hearts
hardened by self-interest and minds dulled with cynicism
we miss the real coming of Christ, let us pray to the Lord.

4.
That we do more ourselves to extend Christ's kingdom to the needy,
the spiritually impoverished, the "hollow men," and the people
still ignorant of Christ's love and peace, let us pray to the Lord.

5.
That in our preparations for Christmas we make practical plans to
bring peace to troubled hearts, hope to the despairing, and love to
the un-loved, let us pray to the Lord.

Celebrant:
Heavenly Father, your son emptied himself, taking the form of a
servant in order to save us. Help us to empty ourselves in this season
of repentance that we may do our part in perfecting the kingdom.

SECOND SUNDAY OF ADVENT

Celebrant:
The Christian life is a constant celebration of Advent: God's kingdom is "near", "on the way", always in the process of becoming. John the Baptist challenges us across the centuries to act on the word we have heard, to make ready the way of the Lord.

Leader:
For men of power who shape the future of the world: may the Spirit fill them with the gifts Isaiah foretold: wisdom, insight, courage, right judgment, love of God, and reverence for life. We pray to the Lord.

2.
For our civil courts: may men learn to judge not only with their eyes and ears, but with their hearts as well to insure true justice. We pray to the Lord.

3.
For our community, and for Christian communities everywhere: may we constantly search for new and more effective ways to carry on Christ's work of reconciliation among men. We pray to the Lord.

4.
For those who lead us in the Church: may the simplicity of Christ's coming renew them in their dedication to the service of all men. We pray to the Lord.

5.
For ourselves: may we accept one another as God has accepted us, and so be a sign for all the world of Christ's continued presence in our midst. We pray to the Lord.

Celebrant:
Father, John the Baptist warned the so-called "faithful" of his time that their religion was not an excuse for inactivity; that lip-service to you is no replacement for service to one another. Help us this Advent to acknowledge our failings frankly, and to grow in love for you and our fellow man, that Christ may be born again in this world through our lives.

THIRD SUNDAY OF ADVENT

Celebrant:
Our prayers search for good news, for the fulfillment of our needs in a source outside ourselves. Pray today for the insight to find within our lives the way to peace in the Lord.

Leader:
For our church, that the news it transmits to all men will be "acceptance and friendship in Christ Jesus," let us pray to the Lord.

2.
For the people of the world, that they will not sit idly by if their leaders intimidate, harass, and slander their brothers and sisters, let us pray to the Lord.

3.
For all who must ask, "What shall I do? " that they will find gentle and compassionate guides, let us pray to the Lord.

4.
For the strength to live our lives in Christ where there is no threat or fear, no hate or guilt, no time or end, let us pray to the Lord.

5.
For the courage to acknowledge that we are not important enough to change the world all at once, let us pray to the Lord.

Celebrant:
Lord,
guide our consciences so we will hold firmly to your truth and love.
Give us the confidence to open our lives to all men so that they may
know us as Christians, a free people who have chosen your path through
Christ our Lord.

Celebrant:
Knowing by faith that God has already come to us in Jesus Christ,
pray that his kingdom will fully come.

Leader:
For the leaders in Christ's Church, that like Elizabeth, they may be filled
with the Holy Spirit, and recognize where the Lord is at work, we pray to
the Lord.

2.
For the poor, for victims of injustice, for victims of their own sin, for all
who are in despair, that they may discover their leader in Jesus and find
their defense in his followers, we pray to the Lord.

3.
For all who sit in darkness and in the shadow of death, who know neither
Jesus as Lord nor God as their Father, that they will recognize in this
community the love that God has for them, we pray to the Lord.

4.
.For the people now living in the land of David and Jesus—Jewish, Moslem,
and Christian—that God will raise up for them daring peacemakers to fi-
nally bring about justice, trust, and mutual friendship we pray to the Lord.

5.
For ourselves, that we may believe like Mary that all God's promises to us
will be fulfilled, we pray to the Lord.

Celebrant:
God our Father, we believe as we have heard, that we are sanctified not by
sacrifices of animals, but by the obedience of Jesus your Son. We ask you
to make us obedient to you by helping us follow the Word of the Gospel,
through Christ our Lord.

CHRISTMAS

Celebrant:

No woman, no man need be a stranger to God's Word. God's Word
became one of us. In Jesus, the will of God that makes the world go
'round is sensitive to the slightest human concern. So we ask each other
now in prayer to witness to and plead for the concerns of people everywhere.

Leader:

For all the churches, all communities of faith, that they may manifest the
good news of Jesus in their every breath and act, let us pray to the Lord.

2.

For the governments and leaders of the world, that prophets may be heard
and that prisoners of conscience may be freed, and that the resources of
the world may be turned to serve the poor and lowly, let us pray to the
Lord.

3.

For persons who are in jails, in hospitals, in refugee camps, in places ra-
vaged by war, in ghettos and in slums, that the new creation we celebrate
today may heal and free us all, let us pray to the Lord.

4.

For those who are alone when no one should be alone, that barriers of
fear, suspicion, and mistrust may fall before the love of Jesus, let us pray
to the Lord.

5.

For those of us assembled here to worship the Father, that our thanksgiving
may be echoed faithfully in all our thoughts and words and lives, let us
pray to the Lord.

Celebrant:

Our Father, on this day as we recall Jesus' birth, every woman, man and
child on earth is in our hearts and consciences. Keep every one of them
there always, and let the measure of our lives' success be the peace,
equality, and solidarity we here achieve. Through Christ our Lord.

HOLY FAMILY

Celebrant:
Our Lord chose to share with us the slow schooling of human growth,
in the intimate and first community that is the family. Because we
are called to be God's chosen ones, his family, let us pray simply for
all families.

Leader:
May kindness take lasting root in our lives, making our homes centers of
warmth and peace, let us pray to the Lord.

2.
That parents, recalling the love that gave life to their children, might ad-
monish in patience and wisdom, thankful to God for their sons and daughters, let us pray to the Lord.

3.
That children dedicate themselves to thankfulness, recognizing that
from their parents they receive gifts they can never lose, let us pray to
the Lord.

4.
That brothers and sisters, sharing the life of the same family, might bear
with one another, and that they might recognize that all men are brothers,
let us pray to the Lord.

5.
That the word of God might dwell in our families, let us pray to the Lord.

Celebrant:
Our Father, your Son and our Brother came to teach us mercy and forgiveness. May his Spirit of peace and wisdom draw all men into one family and
bring us home to You.

MARY, MOTHER OF GOD

Celebrant:

We believe that when God chose to call Mary to be the mother of his Son, he made her fully responsive to his call. We pray for ourselves and for all God's church, that we may also be unselfish in responding to his word.

Leader:

We pray for our bishops, for preachers, for theologians, and for all who must interpret God's word and teach it, that as they grow in an understanding of Mary's role she may become a sign not of contradiction but of unity for the Christian churches. For this we pray to the Lord.

2.

For all who are called to tasks that are trying and challenging, that they will be able to answer like Mary with a simple and generous "yes," we pray to the Lord.

3.

For those who are called to lives of celibacy and virginity, that they may find their lives fruitful in the service of others, we pray to the Lord.

4.

For those who are called to marriage, that they will be faithful and honest in sharing their lives and that thus their children by experience will come to have some grasp of the meaning of God's love for us, we pray to the Lord.

5.

For those who are most deeply entangled in sin, that the power of Jesus may transform them, and that they may learn to praise God's grace, we pray to the Lord.

Celebrant:

Our Father, God, we believe that the Son you sent to us is to be king forever. Reform our hearts, so that we will be eager and dedicated in his service like Mary his mother, and will share her confidence and joy. We ask this in Jesus' name.

EPIPHANY

Celebrant:
As God once revealed his Son to the men from the East, he reveals him
anew in every age. We ask him to make Jesus more truly known to us
now.

Leader:
For those of us who know Jesus only as the just Lord who will judge the
living and the dead, that we may recognize that nowhere is greater compassion found than in his judgment, we pray.

2.
For those of us who see Jesus solely as a kindly, loving friend, that we
may recognize the uncompromising demands which his friendship makes
on us, we pray.

3.
That we may see Jesus not only as the child worshiped by the wise men,
but also as our Savior abandoned and dying on Calvary, and risen from the
dead, we pray.

4.
For those who cannot believe in Jesus because they know him only through
the caricatures presented by his enemies and sometimes by his friends.
May they come to know him as he is, we pray.

5.
For the Jewish people who are a special revelation of God and a
glory of the human race, we pray.

Celebrant:
We thank you, Father, for revealing your Son to us as the light by which
we can see the world as it is. Open our eyes to that light, we ask in Jesus'
name.

BAPTISM OF THE LORD

Celebrant:
We confess that Jesus is the Messiah of God, anointed with the Holy
Spirit and with power. We pray that this Spirit will be active among us.

Leader:
That the Lord will send his Spirit upon bishops, priests, writers, and
teachers and on all who are heard by many within the Church, and
make them announce the Gospel boldly and faithfully. For this we
pray.

2.
That the Spirit will come to young mothers, to contemplative nuns, to
students in our schools, and to all the Church to revive a spirit of prayer
and wonder of God's work. For this we pray.

3.
That the Spirit will be in our hearts and his power in our hands, to transform our (parish/convent/community/ . . . .) into a community of love,
which by word and deed will proclaim God's love to all the world.
For this we pray.

4.
That God's consoling and strengthening spirit will come to the victims
of famine and war, to lonely old people, to young people faced with
death, and to all who find their lives in ruins, that they may find meaning
in life and power to change what can be changed. For this we
pray.

5.
That the words we speak and the prayers we make may nourish the
spirit and soul of mankind, for this we pray.

Celebrant:
Father, stir up your Spirit in us, and make us obedient to the Gospel of
your Son. We ask this in Jesus' name and for his sake.

Second Sunday in Ordinary Time, page 30

Second Sunday in Ordinary Time, page 30

ASH WEDNESDAY

Celebrant:
The Prophet Joel urged an oppressed people to seek God's sympathy by
prayer and fasting. Joel's constraint is also ours, a people who live
in anxious and violent times. This is the acceptable time to pray.

Leader:
That the Church, by its own example of sacrifice and sharing, will
help relieve the suffering of the world's poor and hungry and oppressed,
let us pray to the Lord.

2.
For the leaders of our country, and of other countries, that they will be
willing to make extraordinary sacrifices to call a halt to the struggle for
ever more powerful and deadly weapons, let us pray to the Lord.

3.
That the voices of political prisoners, and those who have sought asylum
from making war, will be heeded by those who are responsible for injustice
and repression, let us pray to the Lord.

4.
That during this Lent, God will move us to be less preoccupied with
ourselves and less insensitive to others' needs so we may show
tenderness to the poor and to those among us who are alone, let us
pray to the Lord.

5.
For those who need work and financial assistance, that in our economy
we will find a way to serve all men, let us pray to the Lord.

Celebrant:
Father, teach us to pray and fast in such a way that we do not call
attention to ourselves, but rather grow in faith, in joy, and in
openness to others, through Christ, our Lord.

FIRST SUNDAY OF LENT

Celebrant:
Because we all have different needs we will each be observing Lent in different ways, by prayer, by reading, by fasting, by sharing our time, our money, our talents with those who need us. Let us pray that these things will make us more free to follow Jesus.

Leader:
That we who have followed our mother Eve and our father Adam in sin and selfishness may be converted and live, we pray to the Lord.

2.
That we may be free to listen not only to the scriptures that we like, but to every word that comes from the mouth of God, we pray to the Lord.

3.
For all who lead God's people, that the Lord will enable them to accept the burdens of their ministry with strength and courage, we pray to the Lord.

4.
For leaders of all nations, that they will not worship the gods of wealth or power or prestige, but will serve only the God of the widow and the poor: for this we pray to the Lord.

5.
For those who cannot afford the luxury of Lent: victims of war, of sickness, of drugs, of unspeakable grief or loneliness, whose lives already hold more terror and pain than they can bear, we pray to the Lord.

Celebrant:
We praise you, Lord, as we enter this season. Let our observances broaden our hearts, so that we can look forward with ever greater joy and longing to Holy Easter. We ask this in Jesus' name and for his sake.

SECOND SUNDAY OF LENT

Celebrant:
The Lord has sent his Son to proclaim the Good News of Salvation, the good news that we are all brothers and sisters with God as our Father, and that no person has a right to enslave another.

Leader:
That all men and women may know that they were created for immortality and to become free, unblemished and beautiful in the eyes of their creator, let us pray to the Lord.

2.
That all leaders may learn from Pontius Pilate's example that they must listen to the truth no matter who speaks it, let us pray to the Lord.

3.
That no person will be denied his or her God-given rights, let us pray to the Lord.

4.
That bigots will find love, cowards will find strength, and warriors, peace, let us pray to the Lord.

5.
That the grace and beauty of creation will fill all who feel empty, ugly, or anxious, let us pray to the Lord.

Celebrant:
Lord, you have told us we were created to your image, and yet we are often treated as slaves by those who have power. Free us from the judgments of the unjust, and help us to pursue life courageously in your grace, through Christ our Lord.

THIRD SUNDAY OF LENT

Celebrant:
We celebrate the many gifts of God, especially the cleansing water that brought us to life as sons and daughters of God. Let us pray for all those who may still be strangers to the Good News of Christ, but who are also our brothers and sisters in the Lord.

Leader:
For all who exercise authority in the Church, that they may be open minded to the problems of those under their jurisdiction. We pray to the Lord.

2.
For alcoholics, drug users, unwed mothers, and all those who the world rejects, that Christians may offer them comfort and help. We pray to the Lord.

3.
For all those Samaritans of today who encounter bitterness and rejection in the service of others, that their commitment to love may be stronger than their desire to be loved. We pray to the Lord.

4.
For all who leave their homes and their friends to help people in our own country or in far off lands: as they help others develop, may they themselves grow; as they teach, may they learn. We pray to the Lord.

5.
That we be channels of God's love and healing to those who are wounded in body, mind or spirit. We pray to the Lord.

Celebrant:
Father,
Christ has shown us
that love recognizes no barriers
and waits for no invitation.
Love risks rejection,
reaching out to any and every one in need.
The love of Christ has found us
and impels us to find each other.
Teach us to love as he has loved us.
We ask this, Father, in his name.

FOURTH SUNDAY OF LENT

Celebrant:
My friends, our presence here today reflects commitment to spiritual things—our desire to live the spirit of Christ which is in us. Let us pray with the certainty of Martha and Mary that through Christ we shall rise one day to live in glory with the Father.

Leader:
For the Church of the Spirit that it will guide the world to the rich, loving life of the resurrected, let us pray to the Lord.

2.
For doctors, lawyers, and welfare supervisors, that they never be blind to the Spirit of God in each person they minister to, let us pray to the Lord.

3.
For all who need to see a Lazarus raised from the dead to believe Jesus is the resurrection and the life, let us pray to the Lord.

4.
For artists, composers, inventors, and all men and women who open ways for the Spirit to touch our hearts and minds, let us pray to the Lord.

5.
For all who are considered inferior because they are poor whites, blacks, chicanos, or other ethnic groups, that the Gospel will vindicate them before all men, let us pray to the Lord.

Celebrant:
Lord, you have given us the resurrection and the life, the life that survives death. Support us in our labor to live as concerned men and women proclaiming the spirit of Jesus even though fear and anxiety lurk around every corner, and the disagreements of men are often settled by death.

FIFTH SUNDAY OF LENT

Celebrant:
Puzzled and depressed by the disintegration of life which we see in our world, we turn in prayer to him in whom we live.

Leader:
For those who face death by war, by hunger, or by disease, and for those whose lives are rendered hopeless through injustice without redress, that they may live indeed, we pray to the Lord.

2.
For those whose life is paralyzed by fear, who are unable to laugh or to be angry, to venture any risk, or to love, that they may experience the freedom which God's spirit brings, we pray to the Lord.

3.
For those who are lost in the death of sin, whose lives are choked by their cruelty or callousness or greed or lust or apathy, that they may come to recognize a brother or a sister in every human being, we pray to the Lord.

4.
For those who have departed from us in death, whether they died strong in faith or in confusion and fear, that they may rise in glory with Jesus on the last day, we pray to the Lord.

5.
That we who have been sealed with the Holy Spirit might strive to develop a profoundly Christian life for the service of mankind, we pray to the Lord.

Celebrant:
God our Father, you created your world by your word, and by your breath you gave life to humankind. Speak your word again, and breathe out your Spirit that we may have life. We ask this through Christ our Lord.

PASSION SUNDAY

Celebrant:
Confessing that Jesus is Lord, and marvelling that he became one
of us and died so that we could live, we pray to his father with confidence.

Leader:
For our bishops, our priests, and ourselves that, like Jesus we may be
true friends of the poor and suffering, we pray to the Lord.

2.
That, as Christ did not pride himself on being the Son of God, we
do not pride ourselves on being closer to God than our separated brethren.

3.
That God's revelations to his prophets, may become the Easter reality
for us, we pray to the Lord.

4.
For all who mourn the death of those who were close,
for those who grieve over losses and failures which seem to destroy
their lives, that they may know Jesus as their brother and share his
triumph, we pray to the Lord.

5.
For those whose ideals are high and whose hope is strong, that they
may persevere like Jesus to the end, we pray to the Lord.

Celebrant:
God our Father, since you sent your Son Jesus Christ to search out
and save what was lost, let him find us and all whom he came to save.

HOLY THURSDAY

Celebrant:
Christ established the Eucharist we celebrate today as the new paschal feast with himself as the Lamb. Calling all men to his table to share the freedom of the Father we pray:

Leader:
For the leaders of the world, that they may limit their armaments and seek the peace of Christ, let us pray to the Lord.

2.
For the church, that its Jewish heritage of passover freedom will make it the spokesman for liberty in the world, let us pray to the Lord.

3.
For the sick and the weak, that they may find strength and renewal in the humility of the Teacher and Lord, let us pray to the Lord.

4.
For the unwashed, the filthy, the degenerate, that they may accept the saving gift of the Lamb, let us pray to the Lord.

5.
For all who called themselves Christians but no longer break bread with Christ in the eucharistic banquet, let us pray to the Lord.

Celebrant:
Father we pray for openness to the humble freedom you offer all men through Jesus Christ, your Son. May the Lord's Supper live in our hearts to feed the world around us.

EASTER SUNDAY

Celebrant:
We have heard the testimony of the apostles that Jesus has risen from
death to life. Let us pray that his resurrection may bring new life to the
world.

Leader:
For the Pope, for the bishops, and for all who have roles of leadership
in the Church, that they may be confirmed in their faith, and may
proclaim the risen Christ with power and authority, we pray to the Lord.

2.
For the President, the Congress, the judiciary, and the leaders of all
nations, that by pursuing justice they may bring new life to the world,
we pray to the Lord.

3.
For those whose faith is weak, for those who have grown tired of
believing, for those whose faith is inmature, who are afraid to look at
the world as it truly is lest they be unable to go on believing, that they
may again find their faith in Jesus, who triumphs over death, we pray
to the Lord.

4.
For the miserable of this world, for the lonely, for those who have lost
their loved ones, those who are swamped by debts or by their duties
in life or by frightful problems that are too great for them, that the Lord
who conquers death may give them strength, we pray to the Lord.

5.
For those who go before us in death, that in Jesus they may find peace
and refreshment, and may share his resurrection, we pray to the Lord.

Celebrant:
Jesus, our Lord and our Brother, you gave faith to your friends, who
did not understand the scripture, that you must rise from the dead. Give
such faith to your Church and to your world, that they may be renewed
in hope. We ask it in your name and for your sake.

SECOND SUNDAY OF EASTER

Celebrant:
Jesus stands in our midst and says "Peace."
Is it a question, command, or a gift?
Let us pray that it be realized among us.

Leader:
That our lives be bright with peace and joy because Jesus our Lord
has risen and come into our midst, we pray to the Lord.

2.
That the frightened of the world may rejoice to find God with
them, and the powerful may be inspired to seek him, we pray to
the Lord.

3.
For those who live in darkness and the shadow of death,
for those who live in alleys and doorways, for those who are
trapped by power or position, by stubbornness or uncertainty,
that they may not wait in vain for the coming of the Lord,
we pray to the Lord.

4.
That our pride may yield to the love of God, we pray to the Lord.

5.
For those who live in doubt, and for those who are afraid to believe,
that our Lord may inspire them and that the Church may encourage
them, we pray to the Lord.

Celebrant:
Lord, break through the closed doors of our lives;
bring us to life;
dispel our fears;
make us believers and inheritors of your promise

Celebrant:
We stand before the Father as people who have poisoned the air he gave us to breathe, the water he gave us to drink, the soil he has provided for planting. We have poisoned our relationships with others by our suspicion and violence. In all these things we have poisoned our relationship with God and have thus cut ourselves off from the very source of life. Let us, therefore, pray to the Father that we may be reconciled with our planet, with our brothers, with ourselves.

Leader:
For all who suffer the loneliness of separation, whether by their own decision or someone else's, that they may discover the opportunity for reconciliation, let us pray to the Lord.

2.
For all those who work to purify life in this world, by overcoming chaos, fear, loneliness, and hatred, that through grace they will not stand alone but will be joined by all men, let us pray to the Lord.

3.
For all who choke on the poisoned water, food or air, that they may receive the gifts of time and courage to work for a restored planet, let us pray to the Lord.

4.
For all who feel cut off from the warmth, life and joy of creation, let us pray to the Lord.

5.
For the power of love to really consume us, that we may exercise our ministry of reconciliation with courage and perserverance, let us pray to the Lord.

Celebrant:
Father, a lot of the time we feel cut off from almost everything and everybody. Please let your love enter our brokenness and heal us. Give us the grace to reach out with love and caring to touch the lives of others.

FOURTH SUNDAY OF EASTER

Celebrant:
Let us pray to our Father, who has given us Jesus as our shepherd to care
for the Church, and for the whole world.

Leader:
May the Church of Christ be protected from false pastors, from
thieves who slip in to steal, from those who would lead it for their
own profit or who would lead it astray, and may those who lead it
speak with the voice of Jesus. For this we pray to the Lord.

2.
For men and women of good will who do not know Jesus, that they
may have the joy of recognizing what God has done for them in Christ,
that they may repent and be baptized and receive the gift of the
Spirit, we pray to the Lord.

3.
For those who suffer like Jesus for doing what is right, even if they do
not know his name, we pray to the Lord.

4.
For refugees and prisoners, and for all who must live away from
their homes, for those who are helpless to protect their families
or who suffer persecution or who cannot make any sense out of
their lives, we pray to the Lord.

5.
For us who are gathered today in our Father's house, that we may
recognize Jesus' voice as we share his Sacrament, and that this week
we may grow more ready to sense where he wants to lead us, we pray to
the Lord.

Celebrant:
Our Father, God, we acknowledge that you have raised your Son Jesus
from the dead and made him shepherd of all your Church. We ask you
to make your Church responsive to his call, so that we will attract all our
fellow humans to recognize what you have accomplished for them. We
ask this through Christ our Lord.

FIFTH SUNDAY OF EASTER

Celebrant:
We are a chosen people, a holy nation, a community set apart by God.
But in a society that does not welcome too many questions or tolerate
too many exceptions, we would much rather be like everyone else. So
too, the Apostles. Christ told them he was their way, their truth, their
life—and still they were hoping for an easier way, a more "reasonable"
truth, a more profitable life. Acknowledging our weakness, but profess-
ing our faith, let us pray.

Leader:
That all who have been called to live the Good News of Christ may have
the courage to follow him in the path of service and self-sacrifice: we
pray to the Lord.

2.
That the Christian Church, especially its leaders, may never let the fear
of rejection dissuade them from preaching the gospel, whether its message
be welcome or unwelcome: we pray to the Lord.

3.
That the deacons of the Church may offer our profit-conscious
world the witness of service done solely out of love: we pray to
the Lord.

4.
That singers and actors, t.v. personalities and radio announcers, and all
those people we never meet who offer us the service of entertainment and
information may look beyond financial reward and find satisfaction in
using their talents for the benefit of their brothers: we pray to the Lord.

5.
For those who have discovered in the breaking of bread the joy
of Christ's presence, that they may share that joy with others, we
pray to the Lord.

Celebrant:
Father,
it is never easy to commit oneself to one way, one truth, one life.
It is not easy to follow Jesus Christ.
See in these petitions we place before you today the great desire
of our lives:
to be for one another and for the world all that Christ wants us to be.
We ask this, Father, in his name.

SIXTH SUNDAY OF EASTER

Celebrant:
We live in the cities of this earth bearing the burdens of our confusion and our wars. From every side prophets arise to tell us the meaning of our lives. We pray that we do not lose our vision of the New Jerusalem or become deaf to the whispers of the spirit who speaks to us in the sufferings of men.

Leader:
That empty store fronts, holes in the asphalt, vandalized cars will tell us of our failures in the cities of this world, let us pray to the Lord.

2.
That we will seek peace by reading the facts and searching out the issues, rather than by avoiding them, let us pray to the Lord.

3.
That by not being afraid to listen to angry voices we will begin to hear the sorrow of the human heart, let us pray to the Lord.

4.
That we will not see the solutions we devise for the problems of our cities or country as monuments to our immortality, but only as steps toward better answers, let us pray to the Lord.

5.
For the power of God's love to consume us, that we may exercise our ministry of reconciliation with courage, let us pray to the Lord.

Celebrant:
We stand firm in the life of Christ who tells us again and again, "Do not be afraid" as he was not afraid when he was killed in the name of the common good. The spirit imposes no burdens. The spirit wastes no words. Father come to us. This will be enough.

ASCENSION

Celebrant:
With the apostles we are exhorted by the angel not to stand looking up into heaven, but to prepare the world for Jesus' return. Let us pray that his kingdom will come.

Leader:
For the Church, for its leaders, and its pastors and for all its people, that we will be eager to see that the Good News is preached to every creature, we pray to the Lord.

2.
For missionaries, for teachers, for parents, that what they teach in Christ's name will truly be the Good News which he came to bring, we pray to the Lord.

3.
For men everywhere whose work is exploited for the benefit of a few, for women who are treated as the property of men, for children who grow up without hope, that they may be liberated from oppression and become free to hear God's word, we pray to the Lord.

4.
For people throughout the world who refuse to listen to God's word, who take advantage of their fellow human beings, who are imprisoned in their selfishness or sloth, that they may be converted and live, we pray to the Lord.

5.
For ourselves, gathered here at the Lord's table, that God may convince us that our hope lies not only in that which can be seen, we pray to the Lord.

Celebrant:
God our Father, you have placed Jesus at your right hand not to separate him from us, but so that he can be equally present to us all. Let your Spirit therefore fall upon your Church with power, so that we may experience his presence among us. In Jesus' name we ask it.

SEVENTH SUNDAY OF EASTER

Celebrant:
Christ, who made his Father's name known to the world and who gave us the teaching he received from his Father, prays that we would belong to the Father. We join him in that prayer.

Leader:
That we, like the early Christian community, join in continuous prayer and the sharing of our goods, let us pray to the Lord.

2.
That fear of suffering or ridicule never cause us to be ashamed of belonging to our Father's family, let us pray to the Lord.

3.
That rather than always complaining of our sufferings we realize that we are sharing in the sufferings of Christ, let us pray to the Lord.

4.
That as Christ made the Father's name known to us, we make his name known to the world, let us pray to the Lord.

5.
That at our death, having finished the work the Father has given us to do, we can say with Christ, "Father, the hour has come; glorify your son," let us pray to the Lord.

Celebrant:
Father, as you have glorified Christ when you raised him from the dead prepare us also each day for glorification.

PENTECOST

Celebrant:
Let us pray that the same Spirit who transformed the apostles may breathe new life into his Church.

Leader:
For the people of Christ's Church, that the Spirit may inspire us with new gifts of wisdom and understanding and fortitude, to know what must be done and to do it, we pray to the Lord.

2.
For the leaders of Christ's Church, that they may recognize the Spirit's work, and protect and foster it, we pray to the Lord.

3.
For those who are separated from Christ by sin, by refusal to know and accept themselves, the world, and God's love: that the Spirit may liberate them from narrowness and fear, and may lead them to openness and freedom, we pray to the Lord.

4.
For all who fear self-discipline, that the Spirit may lead them gently into that control of themselves which makes them capable of accomplishing what they truly want, we pray to the Lord.

5.
For the people with power in England and Ireland, in the United States and Southeast Asia, and the Middle East, that they may not resist the Spirit's call for justice and peace, we pray to the Lord.

Celebrant:
God our Father, we ask you to let your Spirit fall on the world again, with all his gifts and a new Pentecost, so that we may know Jesus Christ returning in glory. In Jesus' name.

TRINITY SUNDAY

Celebrant:
Praising the love and the unity of the three Persons in God, let us who
share in the life of the Trinity, ask our Father's help in these our needs.

Leader:
For the Christian Church, that the divisions which plague us from
within and separate us from one another may be healed according
to the model of Trinitarian unity. This we ask praying.

2.
For our president and civil leaders, that God's plan for the unity of
mankind be present in their work and concern for the common good.
This we ask praying.

3.
For all who by race or poverty are trapped in our tortured cities,
that God grant them the hope and the strength to overcome. This
we ask praying.

4.
For our community, that it always see its duty to extend the hand
of friendship to all who are lonely and depressed. This we ask praying.

5.
For a new spirit and a new heart in each of us that our lives may be a
celebration of Christ's new commandment of love This we ask praying.

Celebrant:
God our Father, today we celebrate the Feast of the Holy Trinity
realizing that we must build our Christian community in the image
of this great mystery. Help us to love others as you, the Son and
Spirit have loved us, and give us the strength to proclaim this
message to all.

CORPUS CHRISTI

Celebrant:
Lord, we spend a lot of time today looking at all kinds of bodies. Bodies that are beautiful, or exciting, or inviting, or comforting. On TV we see overweight bodies. We see starving bodies. We see torn bodies. We see broken bodies. We see busy bodies. God put his love in a body. We need to know more about it.

Leader:
For the courage to taste the body and blood of Christ—his life, his self-giving, his caring, his reaching, his touching, his vulnerability, his healing, let us pray to the Lord.

2.
For the knowledge that if Jesus was only man, he saved no one but himself; and if he was only God, his drama did not really touch my humanness. Let us pray to the Lord.

3.
For strength to work toward building the body of Christ twelve ways stronger. Let us pray to the Lord.

4.
For those who give us strength in making bread, in reaching out and supporting us, let us pray to the Lord.

5.
For ourselves, that we will have the courage to be the body of Christ, by our caring, our loving, our involvements, with our brothers and sisters, let us pray to the Lord.

Celebrant:
Lord, lay your grace upon us, that the body of Christ may not be to us the substance of our isolation and uncaring, but our encounter with life and love. Amen.

SACRED HEART

Celebrant:
My brothers and sisters, in this age of science we do well to recall the place of the heart in literature and legend. Through every generation the heart is the symbol of man's deepest loves and hates, the part of him most sensitive to his world. We remember that since Calvary, the heart of Christ is the symbol of self-sacrificing love and the promise of eternal life.

Leader:
For simple hearts, straining beneath the burden of unemployment, poor housing, and other people's wars: may our country's laws, resources and people help them to reaffirm their dignity and rebuild their lives. We pray to the Lord.

2.
For believing hearts, who lift themselves to the Lord in worship: may they reach out to serve the Lord as he lives in his people. We pray to the Lord.

3.
For bitter hearts, who sneer at love and shut themselves off from others: may the Spirit of Christ alive among us open them again to the goodness of man. We pray to the Lord.

4.
For young hearts, searching for a love and a life worthy of their total dedication: may they look beyond the gods of affluence to the heart of Christ and a life lived for others. We pray to the Lord.

5.
For doubting hearts, who cannot see Christ in his Church or life in his gospel: may there be Christians whose love will renew their faith, whose lives will inspire them to action. We pray to the Lord.

Celebrant:
Father, we are the people who have broken the heart in Christ. Help us to become again the "little ones" Christ speaks of in the gospel: the gentle of heart, proclaiming with our lips and our lives the infinite power of love. We ask this through Christ our Lord.

SECOND SUNDAY IN ORDINARY TIME

Celebrant:
"Light," "Lamb", "grace," "peace"—the Jesus through whom our faith commits us to be always becoming new persons is so described today. His kingdom is unbounded by our laws and habits, and is clean contrary to our systems. So we pray for one another, sisters and brothers, that this "little while" may be a very little while and that his kingdom come.

Leader:
That the light of Jesus may warm as well as instruct us in the worth of every single one of us . . . and of all people, let us pray to the Lord.

2.
That the peace of Jesus may be our only chosen weapon in the struggle for the new creation, let us pray to the Lord.

3.
That the Lamb of God may stir our blood to sacrifice whatever separates us from the outcasts and oppressed of our community, let us pray to the Lord.

4.
That grace, the favor of a loving God, may echo in our public and our private lives, let us pray to the Lord.

5.
That we may follow Jesus rather than our laws and customs, not just in words but in the quality of our lives and deeds, let us pray to the Lord.

Celebrant:
Grant, Almighty God, that we who follow Jesus in his prayers may follow him in other deeds as well, reaching out a reconciling hand to all whom we put down, exclude, and segregate. Through Christ our Lord.

THIRD SUNDAY IN ORDINARY TIME

Celebrant:
Today the scriptures confront us with the tension that has always been a part of Christianity. On one hand, we have seen a great light: Christ is among us. On the other hand, he works in today's world through our hands and hearts—and different people have different ideas as to how Christ should be made known. Aware of the rich insights our diversity can produce, but aware also of its danger, let us pray:

Leader:
For openness on the part of the leaders of the Church: may they realize that unity is not mere uniformity, but the loving use of our many gifts for the good of mankind, let us pray to the Lord.

2.
For the United Nations: may they have the courage and love to continue their work of reconciling the divergent interests of powerful men, let us pray to the Lord.

3.
For the men of power in our own country: may their differing views on the needs of the people never become an excuse for poverty, racism, unemployment, or injustice, let us pray to the Lord.

4.
For parents and children: may parents try to understand the "different-ness" of their children; and may children try to appreciate the views and concerns of their parents, let us pray to the Lord.

5.
For those who feel broken and divided within themselves: may someone's Christ-like love bring healing unity and peace of mind, let us pray to the Lord.

Celebrant:
Father, we believe that the Light has come and lives among us. May that Light, the Christ of Love, be the source of our love for one another. Let our loving unity be a sign to the world that he still lives.

FOURTH SUNDAY IN ORDINARY TIME

Celebrant:
We live in a time when the rhetoric of leadership and the rhetoric of advertising constantly assault the values given us in the gospels. We pray to the Lord that we may experience his goodness, his happiness, his prosperity and his peace.

Leader:
For our church leaders that their first ministry will be to all who need help, especially those whom the world labels weak, let us pray to the Lord.

2.
For government officials and successful businessmen that they will compete to be gentle and merciful, and find fulfillment in peacemaking, let us pray to the Lord.

3.
For parents, that they will freely bring their children love and support without driving them to be "quicker than", "smarter than", or "better than " their peers, let us pray to the Lord.

4.
For young people that they will dare to hunger and thirst for what is right; that they will make peace or be persecuted in the cause of what is right, let us pray to the Lord.

5.
For those who experience life as a disaster, that they may soon discover new life in Christ, let us pray to the Lord.

Celebrant:
Lord,
happiness continues to elude most of us:
to totally trust in you and in each other is a difficult act of faith.
Give us the strength to honestly face the common,
the contemptible, and all you have chosen, through Christ our Lord.

FIFTH SUNDAY IN ORDINARY TIME

Celebrant:

My brothers and sisters, the Lord demands that we each shine our light before all men. Beacons of praise, we can illuminate a starless sky, so the world will never know darkness again. How often does the world seem dark, peopled by masses who cannot sparkle without rhinestones. Give your praise now to the Father.

Leader:

For the Church, that its light will shine in every corner of the world, warming the naked, feeding the starved, and comforting the lonely, let us pray to the Lord.

2.

For the leaders of the world, that their words will glow with truth, love, and reconciliation, let us pray to the Lord.

3.

For our brothers and sisters who filter their light with drugs and alcohol, that they will once again allow themselves to feel their full strength, let us pray to the Lord.

4.

For put-down, stepped on, squelched children exiled to live in dark caverns, that they will survive, let us pray to the Lord.

5.

For men and women confined in jails, institutions, and ghettos, let us pray to the Lord.

Celebrant:

Lord, our gray planet would shine like the sun if our only fear was the fear of your judgment. In this eucharist help us feel your closeness so that the light of our love for all your created will illuminate the world.

SIXTH SUNDAY IN ORDINARY TIME

Celebrant:
We do not gather as a people rich in this world's power, but as a community entrusted with the wealth of God's secret wisdom: a wisdom inspiring in its love but frightening in its challenge; a wisdom which frees the human spirit only when we give our all. Let our prayer today be for faithfulness to the difficult words of Christ:

Leader:
That we may never dismiss another as worthless, but strive always to see the good, the beautiful, the heroic in every human being, let us pray to the Lord.

2.
That the men and women who lead our world will come to learn the wisdom of God, to realize how much they gain by sharing with others, and how powerful they can be when they make peace with their enemies, let us pray to the Lord.

3.
That those who have grown bitter and unhappy in their marriage may find the faith to fall in love with each other again, and discover again in one another new meaning for their lives, let us pray to the Lord.

4.
That the ministers of the Church may witness to the fact that the love of Christ is not limited or bound by the letter of any law, let us pray to the Lord.

5.
That all who have been separated from each other by hate, war, exile, or illness may look beyond today to spring and Christ and new beginnings, let us pray to the Lord.

Celebrant:
Father, we thank you for the continuing presence of Christ among us: and for the way in which he still demands that we put aside our masks, our prejudices, our proper-ness, and begin the difficult but liberating task of learning to love each other. Help us to love. We ask this in his name.

SEVENTH SUNDAY IN ORDINARY TIME

Celebrant:
Let us present our needs to the Father,
asking that he may bless the seed and soil of our lives
with fruitfulness.

Leader:
That those who preach and teach the Word of God may learn to
trust more and more in the power of that Word, we pray.

2.
That the Church may always hear the word of the kingdom with
understanding and welcome it with joy, we pray.

3.
That the resources of our country may be more equitably distributed
among all our citizens and shared with the needy throughout the world,
we pray.

4.
That those who have gone before us in death may share fully in
the freedom and glory of the children of God, we pray.

5.
That those whose lives and words have taught us to believe may
reap the reward of their planting, we pray.

Celebrant.
Father we praise you for having made our lives the fertile soil in
which the Word of your Son has been sown. Keep us true to your
Word, so that we may yield a rich harvest of goodness and love.

EIGHTH SUNDAY IN ORDINARY TIME

Celebrant:
Although the Holy Spirit speaks to the world today, he remains hidden so that we may be his voice and proclaim God's good news of salvation.

Leader:
That we may be disciples of Christ, eagerly and humbly learning the truth of God's loving concern for us, let us pray to the Lord.

2.
That we be followers of Christ every step of our earthly journey and thus be led to his kingdom, let us pray to the Lord.

3.
That we be witnesses to God's love, even though it entail suffering, rejection and martyrdom, let us pray to the Lord.

4.
That we be prophets of the Lord, proclaiming in word and deed the wondrous works of God, let us pray to the Lord.

5.
That we be apostles of Jesus Christ, teaching the wisdom of God and leading men back to their Heavenly Father, let us pray to the Lord.

Celebrant:
Heavenly Father, cleanse our hearts and our lips and give us humility and courage so that we may faithfully answer your call to build your kingdom. We ask this through Christ our Lord.

NINTH SUNDAY IN ORDINARY TIME

Celebrant:
Let us with confidence draw near to the throne of grace, that we may find mercy in time of need.

Leader:
That the leaders in Christ's Church will understand how to obey his injunction not to lord it over others, we pray to the Lord.

2.
For our Congress, our courts, and our President, that they restore confidence in government and exercise their power justly and effectively, we pray to the Lord.

3.
For nations which are subject to harsh, domineering, and tyrannical rule, that they may be liberated, we pray to the Lord.

4.
For the leaders of our communtiy, that they may find means of making life more human and satisfying for our citizens, we pray to the Lord.

5.
That our friends who have gone before us in death will have peace and life in God's presence, we pray to the Lord.

Celebrant:
God our Father, we believe that your Son came to serve and to give his life as ransom for many, and so we ask you to give us freedom and hope through Christ our Lord.

TENTH SUNDAY IN ORDINARY TIME

Celebrant:
Today we pray for faith, the faith of Abraham who left home and
security for an unknown land; for faith that holds out against hope.
Like Abraham we are asked to believe foolishly, for it is the same
God who speaks deep in the heart of us, calling us beyond the
gates of everyday.

Leader:
For puzzled, uncomprehending Christians, that they may learn
that one gesture of mercy is worth a thousand sacrifices,
Lord, hear our prayer.

2.
For the powerful of the world, that they may be confounded by
the faith that moves mountains and the mercy that plants the
Lord in their midst today, Lord, hear our prayer.

3.
For the leaders of nations, that they will learn the power of
extending mercy, love, and forgiveness to enemies, Lord, hear
our prayer.

4.
For the outcasts of the human community, that they will know
mercy, not pity, and that the "faith" of others will give substance
to their hopes, Lord, hear our prayer.

5.
That traditions of peace and non-violence may become rooted in our
way of life, Lord, hear our prayer.

Celebrant:
We would pray for faith, Lord, but perhaps we are not yet ready to
carry such burden, to listen always for your voice calling us beyond
ourselves. And what do we know of mercy? We who have so much
are also arrogant and blind to life around us. Though we are afraid,
we pray boldly to be shattered like Abraham. Amen.

ELEVENTH SUNDAY IN ORDINARY TIME

Celebrant:
We believe that God loved us even when we did not love him, and came to look for us when we were not yet seeking him. Let us pray that having found us he will never let us go.

Leader:
For the Church, that God will send laborers into the field, knowing the authority that Jesus has given them to cast out demons, to heal the sick, and to raise the dead, we pray to the Lord.

2.
For our parish, that we will hear God's word ever better, understand it more deeply, and have the courage to carry it out, we pray to the Lord.

3.
For our President, for our Congress, for our judges, and for those who seek office, that we may be led by persons who are striving for justice and peace, we pray to the Lord.

4.
For those among us who are fathers, and for the fathers of all among us, that the younger ones may live up to their vocation, that the older ones be forgiven their mistakes and enjoy the fruit of their efforts, and that those who have passed on may enjoy their reward, we pray to the Lord.

5.
For victims of cruelty, injustice, and neglect in our city and in all the world, that we may recognize their need and help them, we pray to the Lord.

Celebrant:
God our Father, we know that your Son Jesus has chosen us as he chose his apostles and called each of them by name. Grant us the strength to do the work you have called us to. We ask this through Jesus Christ our Lord.

TWELFTH SUNDAY IN ORDINARY TIME

Celebrant:
Christ was rejected by the establishment of his day, by the civil and religious authorities. We who are rejected identify with Christ.

Leader:
That the many rejections we suffer in our lives may not discourage us but turn us to Christ, the one who does not reject us, let us pray to the Lord.

2.
That those who feel a loss of self-identity will find themselves as brothers and sisters of Christ, let us pray to the Lord.

3.
For the outcasts, the refugees and the political prisoners of the world, let us pray to the Lord.

4.
That we see the image and likeness of God in other people, whether they be Jew or Greek, slave or free, male or female, let us pray to the Lord.

5.
That in taking up our cross each day with Christ we will lose our life so that we may save it, let us pray to the Lord.

Celebrant:
Father, we know that you have created us out of your love. Help us to know you better, for the more we know you the more we know ourselves.

THIRTEENTH SUNDAY IN ORDINARY TIME

Celebrant:
Violence and senseless destruction seem to be the only news we
hear. We ask: Why? And God's answer to us through Jesus is:
have faith in the vision of peace and love you see, and by your
faith make that dream a reality. We gather a broken world into
our thoughts as we pray:

Leader:
For all whose lives have been scarred by the violence of others, that
men and women of vision will touch their lives with love and give them
reason to love again. We pray to the Lord.

2.
For the young, that they will have the courage to face the world as it
really is, while never losing faith in what man can be. We pray to the
Lord.

3.
For those who have grown convinced of man's basic brutality, that the
Spirit open their eyes to see the Christ who lives in every man. We pray
to the Lord.

4.
For those who serve in public office, that they never accept as normal
the violence of poverty and discrimination in our land. We pray
to the Lord.

5.
For the leaders of the Church, that they continually call the Christian
community to serve the needs of all the world, asking no privilege or
reward in return. We pray to the Lord.

Celebrant:
God, our Father, in Christ you have shown us how to face the violence
and evil that lives in our world. He experienced at first hand all that is
worst in man's nature, yet died with a prayer for his killers and rose to
set all men free. Keep his vision of love alive in our hearts. And keep
his faith in the goodness of man alive in the world through our lives.

FOURTEENTH SUNDAY IN ORDINARY TIME

Celebrant:
In Jesus, God reveals himself as one of the little people, a carpenter
from Nazareth, a wandering preacher whose relatives thought him
mad; but we confess him the wisdom of God and the power of God.
Let us pray for little people, that God may defend them.

Leader:
For victims of war, caught in the conflicts of people with power, that they
may have peace, we pray to the Lord.

2.
For the people of small and weak nations, that they may have the prudence
to turn the manipulations of the great governments to their true advantage,
we pray to the Lord.

3.
For those who are economically vulnerable, for migrant workers, and
small businessmen, and unskilled workers, and those who must receive
welfare, that they may have a fair share in the wealth of our nation in
proportion to their needs and their contribution to the common good, we
pray to the Lord.

4.
For those who are politically weak, disorganized, unable to make themselves heard, that their discontent may not be exploited, but that their
needs may be heeded and answered, we pray to the Lord.

5.
For those who are so often rejected by our society, for prisoners, for the
emotionally disturbed, for alcoholics, for drug addicts, for the physically
handicapped, for the retarded, that they may have friends to help them,
we pray to the Lord.

Celebrant:
Lord, you know the needs of your people: hear and answer us through
Christ our Lord.

FIFTEENTH SUNDAY IN ORDINARY TIME

Celebrant:
Our concern for the environment gives us a special appreciation for
the parable in today's gospel. Ecology tells us how difficult it may
become to make things grow. Christ tells us the same thing: the
Spirit of God must work in and through the people to produce that
harvest of faith, hope, and love that can renew the face of the earth.
Let us gather to our hearts all whose lives are touched by the word
of God:

Leader:
For bishops, priests, deacons and all those specially commissioned with the
task of sowing the word of God in men's hearts: may their own living witness help that word grow to fruitfulness. We pray to the Lord.

2.
For those who cannot bear to hear the word of God and for those who choose
to ignore it: may the power of the Spirit and the love of Christians move them
to listen again. We pray to the Lord.

3.
For those whose faith in Christ is tried by persecution or overwhelmed by
personal problems: may they receive encouragement and strength from their
fellow Christians. We pray to the Lord.

4.
For those whose first concern is themselves, who consider their faith a
burden, or who submerge their Christianity beneath the worries of prestige, we pray to the Lord.

5.
For those whose marriage has fallen apart, that they will be able to
rebuild their life, we pray to the Lord.

Celebrant:
Father,
so often we are like those who first heard Christ:
blind, deaf, insensitive to the reality before us.
Help us as we struggle to grasp the word we have listened to,
as we strive to share with others the love we have felt in our midst.
Let Christ grow in our lives.
We ask this, Father, in his name: Christ our Lord.

SIXTEENTH SUNDAY IN ORDINARY TIME

Celebrant:
God has taught us, the book of Wisdom relates, that the virtuous man
is kind to his fellowman. We will pray that our hearts be open to the
word of the Spirit and bear fruit in kindness.

Leader:
That we reflect the kindness and compassion of Christ in all our
contacts with our fellowman, let us pray to the Lord.

2.
That courtesy, a sign of our love, be always evident in our dealings
with both friends and strangers, let us pray to the Lord.

3.
That the good seed of wisdom which the Spirit sows in our hearts
not be choked off by the details and worries of our daily living, let
us pray to the Lord.

4.
That we be sensitive to the feelings, needs and weaknesses of others,
in whom we see Christ himself, let us pray to the Lord.

5.
That we never reject anyone by our hardness of heart, but always be
a refuge for the lonely, the outcast, the timid, the alien, the underprivileged and the derelicts of society, let us pray to the Lord.

Celebrant:
Father, most just and lenient toward us, help us truly to pray with
the Spirit, for then we will pray with love for you and all your people.

SEVENTEENTH SUNDAY IN ORDINARY TIME

Celebrant:
In Jesus Christ, God has become like us. Let us pray that we may become something like God in freedom, in love, in the willingness to give ourselves.

Leader:
For persons of understanding who can discern between good and evil to govern this great people wisely, without exploiting our prejudices and fears and passions, we pray to the Lord.

2.
For those who govern the Church, for teachers and parents and all in roles of influence, that they may have the sense and the courage to present fresh, new wisdom without depriving us of the old, we pray to the Lord.

3.
That the word of God will come with such clarity and power that we will recognize the price we must pay to be faithful to it, and will have the strength to pay what it costs, we pray to the Lord.

4.
For those in crisis who find they must give up everything, family, security, reputation, freedom, if they are to follow Christ, that they may do so in wisdom, and in joy at finding Christ, we pray to the Lord.

5.
For people who are happy, who are in love, for those who are exhilarated with beginning a new life or content in their old life, that their happiness may be a pledge of the joy which cannot fail, we pray to the Lord.

Celebrant:
Father, make us grow more and more to resemble your Son, so that we may be recognized as his sisters and brothers and lead others to love him. We ask this in Jesus' name.

EIGHTEENTH SUNDAY IN ORDINARY TIME

Celebrant:
Brought together in one Spirit by Christ, we stand in the presence of the Father as brothers and sisters. Let us bring together in our prayer today the needs of all who share with us the mystery of human life.

Leader:
That those who lead us in faith work within the Church and within society to heal, unite, and reconcile in love: let us pray to the Lord.

2.
That world leaders renounce hostility born of the drive for power, and lead their nations from self-interest to concern for our common earth: let us pray to the Lord.

3.
That those involved in prison reform, women's rights, and justice for minority races will have the courage to continue their work of education and reconciliation: let us pray to the Lord.

4.
That married couples, parents and children, friends far and near will find time this summer to renew their sharing in love: let us pray to the Lord.

5.
That our family of faith be to our community a sign of Christ's compassion and concern for all: let us pray to the Lord.

Celebrant:
Father,
there is no joy that does not come from your hand,
no pain that does not echo in your heart.
See our needs and give us strength
to work with you and with each other
in building a world where love can live.
We ask this through Christ our Lord.

NINETEENTH SUNDAY IN ORDINARY TIME

Celebrant:
By faith, Peter was able to walk on water. By faith, says Christ, we can move mountains. Let us pray that our faith not falter.

Leader:
For all people whose faith has been shaken by scandal, injustice, disappointment, or someone's death, let us pray to the Lord.

2.
For all people who are looking for a faith, looking for someone to believe in, that they may find Jesus Christ, let us pray to the Lord.

3.
That we be alert to the approach of the Lord, who will come, as he did to Elijah, not in a hurricane, an earthquake, or fire, but in a tiny whispering sound, let us pray to the Lord.

4.
That faith in the constant presence of Christ keep us unafraid in the personal storms in our lives, let us pray to the Lord.

5.
That our faith be alive with the good works without which it is dead, let us pray to the Lord.

Celebrant:
Father, help us, so often of little faith, realize that we are only truly rich when we are rich in faith, for only those steadfast in the faith inherit your kingdom.

TWENTIETH SUNDAY IN ORDINARY TIME

Celebrant:
Brothers and sisters, God has given each of us, even the poorest, some wealth for which we are responsible—our lives, the dignity and feelings of others, our earth, this community. Let us pray that we might be faithful to this trust.

Leader:
For those in authority, that they will not abuse their power or forget that it is primarily for the service of others, let us pray to the Lord.

2.
Knowing how much we have received, may we remember to thank God as well, let us pray to the Lord.

3.
And knowing how much we owe to our fellow men, may we be generous to all with whom we meet, we pray to the Lord.

4.
That we might be trusted in all those small things of the heart, the little debts of every day, let us pray to the Lord.

5.
And that we may wisely use the things of this world, not pursuing elusive wealth of material or of opinion, let us pray to the Lord.

Celebrant:
O God, your Son gave himself so that we might give ourselves in your love. By your Spirit may we become worthy stewards of this one truth by which you would have all men saved.

TWENTY—FIRST SUNDAY IN ORDINARY TIME

Celebrant:
The scripture we have heard today responds with joyful surprise to the
way in which God has called us to himself. "How deep is God's wisdom
and knowledge? Who can understand his decisions? Who can explain his
ways?" Who could have predicted that simple people—those first disciples—
would respond to Christ's faith in them with such complete faith in him?

Leader:
For everyone whose faith rests in Christ and on the living witness of those
who first believed in him: may our profession of faith be made perfect by
lives of love. We pray to the Lord.

2.
For the bishops of the Church: may they recognize and welcome in all
areas of the Christian community the Spirit's gift of leadership. We pray
to the Lord.

3.
For those young people who feel themselves drawn to the message and
personality of Jesus: may we be willing to welcome their enthusiastic witness and may they be willing to share it with us. We pray to the Lord.

4.
For married couples whose lives are a sign of God's intimate love for his
people: may their faith in Christ and in each other renew in those around
them a living faith in God and man. We pray to the Lord.

5.
For the elderly whose lives bear witness to undaunted faith: may they
have friends of all ages to offer them the thanks of respect, security, and
conversation. We pray to the Lord.

Celebrant:
Father,
we praise your infinite goodness
which has given us faith in more than the material goods around us,
which summons us to hope that transcends what we are,
which challenges us to love someone besides ourselves.
Make us equal to this life you have invited us to share.

Twenty-First Sunday in Ordinary Time A 49

TWENTY–SECOND SUNDAY IN ORDINARY TIME

Celebrant:
The scriptures we have shared today have a disturbing challenge to a society that strives for conformity. We are reminded again that God has called us in Christ to be different, to be Christ-like, and this call demands nothing less than the total gift of ourselves. Let us pray for the faith to understand this challenge and the courage to meet it.

Leader:
For all who form the holy Church of God: may we not pattern ourselves on the greed and self-seeking of worldly values, but on the generosity and selfless love of Christ. We pray to the Lord.

2.
For all whose dedication to the Word of God brings them insult and persecution: may the example of Christ and our prayerful support keep them true to the faith they share with us. We pray to the Lord.

3.
For those who search for a love that demands nothing of themselves: may the example of Christians be an inspiration to them to open themselves to the risk of sharing love. We pray to the Lord.

4.
For workers the world over: may they look beyond material reward to see their work as the expression of a God-given personality and their gift to the family of man. We pray to the Lord.

5.
For all who are travelling: may they enjoy the company of their family and friends and return to their homes in safety. We pray to the Lord.

Celebrant:
Father, see our human weakness that drives us to enrich ourselves without a thought for others. But see, too, our faith in Christ and our desire to live as he taught us in the gospel. Help us grow into people who can love as he loved: freely sharing with others the gifts of personality and skill you have given us. We ask this through Christ, our brother and our Lord.

TWENTY—THIRD SUNDAY IN ORDINARY TIME

Celebrant:
Gathered in Jesus' name we pray with confidence to our Father
because we know he will hear our prayers.

Leader:
That parents and teachers, priests and bishops may have wisdom to
know what things to correct and what to ignore, and have the
sensitivity to make their corrections at the right time and with tact,
we pray to the Lord.

2.
That candidates for public office will be responsible and fair in presenting
their own programs and in criticizing their opponents, we pray to the
Lord.

3.
For ourselves and our families to grow in the love which fulfills the
law because love does no evil, we pray to the Lord.

4.
For parents with sick children and people who have lost their job and
for all who are in trouble, that they may find someone to help and
console them, we pray to the Lord.

5.
For those persons who have injured us and those whom we have injured,
that we may be reconciled, we pray to the Lord.

Celebrant:
Father, Jesus said that he is wherever two or three of us are gathered
in his name. Well, here we are all of us gathered in his name, so hear and
answer us for Jesus' sake.

TWENTY—FOURTH SUNDAY IN ORDINARY TIME

Celebrant:
The ability to forgive is perhaps the trait we most associate with our
Lord Jesus Christ. Yet we who profess to follow him seem to
find it such a total contradiction of our human nature. We fear
the loss of our pride, of our "righteousness," of our power over
others in forgiveness. But we are reminded today that only if we
can forgive others will we be forgiven ourselves. And so we pray:

Leader:
For those whose philosophies make us question our Christian values
and tempt us to doubt our faith: may God open their hearts to
faith in Christ. We pray to the Lord.

2.
For those who persecute our brothers and sisters in Christ and
strive to extinguish their faith: may God open their hearts to love.
We pray to the Lord.

3.
For those who would rather go to war than compromise their
personal interests: may God open their hearts to peace. We pray to
the Lord.

4.
For those who pollute our air and water with no thought but their
own profit or enjoyment: may God open their hearts to concern
for others. We pray to the Lord.

5.
For those who have grown bitter over the weaknesses of others: may
God open their hearts to hope in man's goodness. We pray to the Lord.

Celebrant:
Father, we gather to our hearts all who have wronged us and all who
make our lives difficult, whether consciously or not. You have told
us that only by forgiving are we forgiven. Help us grow in the ability
to forgive others and in the humility to see our own faults. As
your love embraces all mankind, so may ours in Christ our Lord.

TWENTY—FIFTH SUNDAY IN ORDINARY TIME

Celebrant:
Each person who works in the vineyard of God's world must bear
burdens that can really be borne by no one else. Let us pray for those
whose burdens are heavy, that they will not lose heart.

Leader:
We pray for those older people who feel neglected or unappreciated
for what they have done, or feel cheated of opportunities that are
open only to a new generation, that they may also be pleased to
see some of their work bearing fruit. For this we pray to the Lord.

2.
For those young people who are indignant at seeing power used
unfairly against them, and ideals being ignored in practice, that they
may not become bitter, but may be driven to work harder and more
effectively for a world of justice and love, we pray to the Lord.

3.
For people in between who feel frustrated, who feel that their fears
are ignored and their voices drowned out by more strident cries, that
their true needs may be met, we pray to the Lord.

4.
For people of all ages who are content or enthusiastic or determined,
that their mood may give hope to others, we pray to the Lord.

5.
For ourselves, so quick to judge and so slow to see our faults, that God
open our hearts to see ourselves, we pray to the Lord.

Celebrant:
We know, Lord, that our thoughts are not your thoughts, nor our
ways yours, and so we ask you not only to answer these prayers of
ours, but also to grant us the gifts we have not had the wisdom to
ask, through Christ our Lord.

TWENTY—SIXTH SUNDAY IN ORDINARY TIME

Celebrant:
Pray, sisters and brothers, for those who need what we possess and for those who possess what we need. Pray that we may not turn deaf ears to these harsh scripture words, but that our lives and our resources may be aimed at an end of both rich and poor—reconciled in your kingdom's equality and solidarity.

Leader:
For the churches and the humble signs of unity we have in our pope and our bishop, that we preach and live to make the human family one in sharing everything, we pray to the Lord.

2.
For those in governmental power and influence, that world and national economies be geared to human needs rather than to greed and profit, we pray to the Lord.

3.
For cooperatives of every kind and all means of social ownership, that we may build structures and institutions in our daily lives more friendly to the gospel, we pray to the Lord.

4.
For community organization in city, neighborhood, and parish, that no one among us may be in want unless we are all in want, we pray to the Lord.

5.
For this congregation, that the sharing and the solidarity we here express and celebrate may be real in all of our relations, we pray to the Lord.

Celebrant:
It is not easy, God, to pray that we may bridge the great abyss between the rich and poor. Our comfort may depend upon that great abyss. So free us and strip us, and make our wills and action the accomplices of your reconciling Spirit. Through Christ our Lord.

TWENTY–SEVENTH SUNDAY IN ORDINARY TIME

Celebrant:
Peter Maurin, a holy man of modern times, said that when it comes to entering the eternal kingdom it is not some clever manipulator, but Christ who calls the shots.

Leader:
That communists and fascists, the proletariat and the capitalist, the government and the loyal opposition, the majority and the minority, the powerful and the weak all work for God's own peace, which is beyond all understanding, let us pray to the Lord.

2.
That in building the kingdom of peace we never reject Christ, who must be the keystone of the structure, let us pray to the Lord.

3.
That we who desire the kingdom of heaven may become poor in spirit, for theirs is the kingdom of heaven, let us pray to the Lord.

4.
That the powerless of this earth, the poor, the prisoners, the unemployed, those suffering injustice, the aged, the crippled and the blind, may find consolation in Christ's promise to give them the kingdom of heaven, let us pray to the Lord.

5.
That with a fuller trust in the protective and loving fatherhood of God we may dismiss anxiety from our minds, let us pray to the Lord.

Celebrant:
Heavenly Father, with hearts full of gratitude and confidence we ask your never-failing help that we may discover true peace now and possess it forever.

TWENTY–EIGHTH SUNDAY IN ORDINARY TIME

Celebrant:
The light of Christ shines in our midst. God the Father has raised up
our brother Jesus to new life and has made him Lord of all creation.
He places the world in our hands and calls us to share his life with all
men. Let us pray for the faith and love to continue his saving work.

Leader:
For all who call upon God as Father and who acknowledge Jesus as
Lord: may they grow in love to become a source of new hope for the
world, a convincing sign of the new life Christ offers all men, let us
pray to the Lord.

2.
For the leaders of nations: may they dedicate themselves wholeheartedly
to the well-being of their people, conscious of the great dignity Christ
has won for all God's sons and daughters, let us pray to the Lord.

3.
For the men and women of science: may they realize their great
responsibility to develop God's creation to perfection, and may they use
their knowledge to bring peace and plenty to all men, let us pray to
the Lord.

4.
For the poor and rejected of this world: may we see more clearly that
they are God's kingdom among us, Christ's presence among us; and may
Christ work through us to bring them new hope, let us pray to the Lord.

5.
For all of us here, called to live a new life in Christ: may our
determination, our willingness to live for others, bring life and hope to
our community and to our world, let us pray to the Lord.

Celebrant:
Father, with Christ your Son, you have made us your sons and daughters.
Help us to build the world entrusted to our care into the one family of
Jesus Christ. We ask this in his name.

TWENTY–NINTH SUNDAY IN ORDINARY TIME

Celebrant:
Friends, now, as always, is the time for renewal.
It is for strength and direction that we must pray.

Leader:
That twisted thoughts and hollow words may flee the light of day,
and shun the heart of man, we pray to the Lord.

2.
For molders of public opinion—journalists, broadcasters, advertisers,
parents, preachers—that they may learn to seek and speak the Truth
in love, we pray to the Lord.

3.
That we may recognize our sinfulness and weakness, and once
again be converted to the Christ, the Lord of our Lives, we pray
to the Lord.

4.
That our words may burst at the seams and overflow Love and
Truth, we pray to the Lord.

5.
That our actions may give life to the words of Christ, and the lie
to the empty promise of darkness, we pray to the Lord.

Celebrant:
Father, don't desert us.
Evil is near; be nearer.
Be our strength and guide;
our own devices have failed us.

THIRTIETH SUNDAY IN ORDINARY TIME

Celebrant:
We pray to our Father with confidence, not because we are so good
but because he is so good that he has to hear us.

Leader:
For the gift of loving the Lord our God with all our heart and all our
soul and all our mind, we pray to the Lord.

2.
For the grace to love our neighbor as we love ourselves, we pray to
the Lord.

3.
For the family besieged by debt, or bereaved by recent death; for the
laborer who is not a citizen in the land, and for all who are easily exploited,
that they will find protection, we pray to the Lord.

4.
For people we don't like because of the way the look, or because
they have a different life-style from ours; that we may see our
common ground and learn to live together. For this we pray to
the Lord.

5.
For the poor, the rejected, the old, the lonely among us, that they may
feel at home in our midst and may find that their love is needed, we
pray to the Lord.

Celebrant:
God our Father, we do not know how to pray as we ought, but you
know all our needs, so hear and answer us through Christ our Lord.

THIRTY—FIRST SUNDAY IN ORDINARY TIME

Celebrant:
The Lord Jesus carried out his Father's work, knowing that it would cost him his life. Let us pray for all who suffer in the attempt to continue his ministry of service.

Leader:
For all who suffer persecution in carrying out Jesus' work, that they may see God's kingdom come, we pray to the Lord.

2.
For people who are derided for repeating old truths, or are suspected for discovering new truths or rebuked for asking new questions, that our ears and minds may be open to them, we pray to the Lord.

3.
For peace, that avarice, envy, and contempt may no longer lead us into war, we pray to the Lord.

4.
For the leaders in the Churches, that they may be glad to be servants of all, we pray to the Lord.

5.
For the children of our community, that they may feel accepted in Jesus' name, we pray to the Lord.

Celebrant:
God our Father, source of all courage, truth, and love, give us the peace which the world cannot give through Christ our Lord.

THIRTY—SECOND SUNDAY IN ORDINARY TIME

Celebrant:
The eucharist we gather for celebrates life, and yet death is all around us. It tempts us to fear the challenge of life. We cannot minimize, we cannot ignore the reality of death, so we pray:

Leader:
For those who fight destruction from disease in their mind or body: may science guided by the Spirit win the struggle against unnecessary death. We pray to the Lord.

2.
For those who face death for their witness to Christ: may the Gospel be their life's unfailing guide and goal. We pray to the Lord.

3.
For those whose martyrdom is the slow death of loneliness, frustration, and despair: may they look beyond themselves to Christ, their brothers, and life. We pray to the Lord.

4.
For all who are deadened by work too mechanized or too menial: may they rediscover their personhood and their lives. We pray to the Lord.

5.
For ourselves: may we follow Christ in drawing good from evil, concern from indifference, love from hatred, and life from death. We pray to the Lord.

Celebrant:
Father, we are often tempted to think of death, as the end of everything. Christ faced death too, but looked beyond it to life. He gave up his life only so that he could have it back perfect and eternal. By our lives may we create life, restore life, preserve life whole.

THIRTY—THIRD SUNDAY IN ORDINARY TIME

Celebrant:
We live in days marked by the words of the Gospel; by material affluence, abundant stimuli, by overwhelming calamities, and the clamor of many prophets. Let us pray for the discernment we so desperately need to be people of justice.

Leader:
In a time when all things are passing away, may our hearts and labor be given to what is of lasting value. We pray to the Lord.

2.
In a time of upheaval and confusion, may we be granted the serenity to trust in God's power and wisdom. We pray to the Lord.

3.
We ask for humility and discernment that we may not be misled, nor mislead others. We pray to the Lord.

4.
When so many are victims of injustice and disorder, may we learn to live in the service of our brothers. We pray to the Lord.

5.
May our own lives give witness of our trust in the Lord Jesus Christ. We pray to the Lord.

Celebrant:
Father, send again Jesus, the sun of justice, that the earth and its peoples might be healed by the rays of his love and the wisdom of his Spirit.

CHRIST THE KING

Celebrant:
In the end Christ the King will say to us that whatever we did to the
least of his brothers and sisters we did to him. Let us pray for these
least that they may find help.

Leader:
For Christ's brothers and sisters who are hungry and cold and homeless,
that Christians may bring them aid, we pray to the Lord.

2.
That jobs may be found and dignity restored to his brothers and sisters
who cannot or will not find work, we pray to the Lord.

3.
For his brothers and sisters in prison, that Christians will find ways
to give them self-respect and prepare them to live and work in society,
we pray to the Lord.

4.
For Jesus' brothers and sisters who are drug addicts or unwed mothers
or alcoholics, that understanding believers may be there to help them
out of the traps they are caught in, we pray to the Lord.

5.
That Christians may be willing to listen to those who are lonely or
confused or frightened, we pray to the Lord.

Celebrant:
God our Father, let us be among those who do these things so that
when Christ comes in glory we will hear him say, "Come you blessed of
my Father and inherit the kingdom prepared for you from the beginning."
We ask this in Jesus' name.

THANKSGIVING DAY

Celebrant:
As consumers, we are conditioned by our economy never to be satisfied. But God, too, is a fantastic supplier, and we stop and take a sample inventory on this special day for giving thanks.

Leader:
For the smell of new rain, for pumpkins, and Snoopy, for the aroma of homemade bread, for cotton candy, for funny looking animals like giraffes and koalas and human beings; let us give thanks to the Lord.

2.
For the smell of fall in the air, for pay checks, and smoked ribs, for the intricate designs of window frost, and for ice cubes and ice cream; let us give thanks to the Lord.

3.
For clean sheets and peanut butter, and perma-press, and stereo-headphones, for vacations and seat belts, for escalators, and for views from tall buildings, and for red balloons; let us give thanks to the Lord.

4.
For first romances and second romances, for eyes to see colors and ears to hear music and feet to dance, for dissenters and the right to dissent, for black and red and brown power, for pine trees and daisies, for newspapers and sandals and frogs; let us give thanks to the Lord.

5.
For parks and woodsmoke and snow, for the smell of leather, for funny buttons and powerful posters, for pecan pies and long hair and french fries and re-cycling centers, for jet planes and for finding a nearby parking space, for zoos and splashing fountains and rock music and Bach music, let us give thanks to the Lord.

Celebrant:
God, you overwhelm us with your goodness. And we have yet to mention your greatest gift, our brother Jesus!   For these and all your gracious gifts please help us to learn how to live thankfully each day.

Celebrant:
Advent is a season of movement and progress. As believers we will not
accept a philosophy that consists of repeating the same round of life
over and over again. Faith sees life as a struggle toward the coming
of God's kingdom. Pray, then, for one another and for all who
suffer because we are not struggling hard enough.

Leader:
That the Church may be an example as well as a preacher of freedom,
let us pray to the Lord.

2.
That our government and the other governments of the world may soon
recognize and reflect the fact that the human family is now one, indivi-
sible, interdependent, let us pray to the Lord.

3.
That the search for peace may reach and quicken all our consciences,
let us pray to the Lord.

4.
That those who envision a kingdom not of profit but of service may
shape changes in our economy and in our politics, let us pray to the
Lord.

5.
That the neglected and unseen victims of our current social order may
move our hearts to search out persons in this neighborhood who need
our help, let us pray to the Lord.

Celebrant:
Teach us to pray, Almighty God, and by our prayers teach us to live.
Your kingdom come on earth as in heaven. Through Christ our Lord.

SECOND SUNDAY OF ADVENT

Celebrant:
The Lord Jesus came to earth gentle, joyful, like a bridegroom to meet his bride; let us pray that his Church will not disappoint him.

Leader:
Knowing that Jesus loves his Church with love beyond measure, may we respond with our love in return. For this we pray to the Lord.

2.
May he make his Church fruitful, bringing forth daughters and sons in his image, free and unselfish like him. For this we pray to the Lord.

3.
That his Church may be faithful to the Lord, putting nothing and no one in that first place which belongs to Jesus alone, we pray to the Lord.

4.
For newlyweds, and those long married, and those in middle years, that their love, fresh and strong or old and mellow or troubled and unsure, may become an ever brighter sign of Christ's love for his Church, we pray to the Lord.

5.
For those who do not know Christ, that our security in God's love may assure them that they too are loved by God, we pray to the Lord.

Celebrant:
God our Father, gathered at the table of the Lord we ask that the sacrament of his body and blood may bring us certainty of his affection through Christ our Lord.

THIRD SUNDAY OF ADVENT

Celebrant:
As the Lord Jesus was unknown among his people until he was
pointed out by John, so his Church on earth continues his presence
even when he is not recognized. Let us pray for this Church, that is
for ourselves, that we may not lose faith in this task of ours.

Leader:
For the leaders of the Church and all who teach and preach, that like
Jesus they may bring the Gospel to the poor and to those who despair
of salvation, we pray to the Lord.

2.
That we will be a community which gives peace to the restless, the
anxious, and the despondent, we pray to the Lord.

3.
That we will be a Church with vision to bring courage to the fearful
and hope to the cynical, we pray to the Lord.

4.
That we will learn to be at peace among ourselves despite real differences,
so that we can be a sign of hope to the world, pointing out the way
of peace, we pray to the Lord.

5.
For those from among us who have died, that they may know the
warmth of God's life-giving love, we pray to the Lord.

Celebrant:
Stir up your might, Lord Jesus, and come. Give your Church the
power to transform hearts, so that we will serve you now, and praise
you forever and ever.

FOURTH SUNDAY OF ADVENT

Celebrant:
Our God has sent his Son into our world and has involved us in the work
of creation. Let us address our petitions to him, as we prepare for him a
place in our hearts:

Leader:
For the entire Church of God: that we may be a sign of his presence
in modern life. We pray to the Lord.

2.
That God's own wisdom may be the source of the guidance we
receive from our political leaders, our social, and religious leaders.
We pray to the Lord.

3.
For the presence of God in the lives of people: especially those who
are forced into crime, violence, and hate. We pray to the Lord.

4.
That as we again stand at the threshold of the mystery of Christ
coming to the world, we may see in ourselves the need for his presence
and welcome him. We pray to the Lord.

5.
That we will seek the spirit of Christ to influence our relationship with
everyone we meet. We pray to the Lord.

Celebrant:
Father, you hear the prayers of your people.
Open our eyes to the work you accomplish through us.
Give nourishment to our faith that we may welcome your presence
among us in the person of Jesus.
We ask this, Father, through Christ our Lord.

CHRISTMAS

Celebrant:
Jesus himself is a great gift to us, but we ask God to grant us more fully the promises which Jesus represents to us.

Leader:
For our pope, our bishop and for all who lead the Church, that they will be able to preach the Gospel with the simplicity and poverty expressed in the story of Jesus' birth, we pray to the Lord.

2.
For world leaders in our nation and elsewhere, that they will work for peace, we pray to the Lord.

3.
For those who are coming back to the sacraments in this season, that their joy in God's love may be full, we pray to the Lord.

4.
For those who are, like Joseph, unable to protect their loved ones from discomfort and misery, we pray to the Lord.

5.
For those who at this moment have no one to love or be loved by, that they may find them, we pray to the Lord.

Celebrant:
Father, you know the needs of the human heart, for you sent Jesus to be a human like us. We ask you to fulfill our needs, even those which we ourselves do not recognize, through Christ our Lord.

HOLY FAMILY

Celebrant:
The family, primary community in God's kingdom on earth, is a preparation ground for living in love with the communion of saints in heaven.   Let us pray for goodness in all human families.

Leader:
For the family of God throughout the world, that its members learn to live in the unity and love for which Christ prayed at the Last Supper, let us pray to the Lord.

2.
For mothers and fathers, that they have the moral strength and Christian character necessary for the growth of their children in grace, let us pray to the Lord.

3.
For all families separated by hatred, bitterness and pride, that they be happily re-united in the love of Christ, let us pray to the Lord.

4.
For children, that by honoring and obeying their parents and by cheerfully helping all members of the family they contribute to the happiness of home life, let us pray to the Lord.

5.
For families who have lost a beloved member through death, that they live in hope of being together in heaven, let us pray to the Lord.

Celebrant:
Heavenly Father, who created the human family in love, help our families, parents and children, grandparents, aunts and uncles, nieces and nephews, in-laws and relatives, and all members of our earthly communities, never to abandon the love in which they were created.

MARY, MOTHER OF GOD

Celebrant:
We gather here, Lord, to begin a new year. Each of us is an individual, unique in all the world. We believe we are sons and heirs, not slaves. The Universe is the house you have given us to care for, to keep, to live in and to grow in. We ask for the courage to be ourselves—strong and brave and beautiful—sons and daughters who see in this home called Universe your name, your love and your voice. May our response be the praise of a joy-filled life.

Leader:
That all persons who make up the Church will have the courage to be sons, not slaves, let us pray to the Lord.

2.
That our government and business leaders will work to preserve our environment from pollution and decay, let us pray to the Lord.

3.
That we might grow more sensitive to the needs of different people — old men, welfare ladies, babies, freaks — for God shines in everybody's face, let us pray to the Lord.

4.
That all of us here might not give up hope in building a better world for all men, let us pray to the Lord.

5.
That each of us may be mindful of our own need of forgiveness and have the humility to take that first step toward ending a family, business, or neighborhood quarrel, let us pray to the Lord.

Celebrant:
Father, help us to be lifegivers, not death-dealers. We pledge this year to open our eyes and ears to each thing's reality and each man's glory, through Christ our Lord.

EPIPHANY

Celebrant:
The entire world is a revelation of God. Let us pray that we will
open our hearts to those people who come to us as strangers with strange
thoughts and strange expressions. Let us pray that we will be curious
about the world and open to all the new ideas and inventions which
come to light every day.

Leader:
That we will not hide our talents in the name of shyness, but will put
our light on the mountaintop for everyone to see, let us pray to the Lord.

2.
That we will neither reduce life's complexity to getting ahead nor
think that personal success is the key to civilization, let us pray to
the Lord.

3.
That we will learn to see in the poor, the diseased and the suffering,
the image of God, let us pray to the Lord.

4.
That we who are afraid and alone may get the courage and grace to
face the great things that are happening in the world, let us pray to
the Lord.

5.
That we may embrace the people and the cultures of Asia because they
are part of ourselves and a revelation of the same spirit who breathes
in us, let us pray to the Lord.

Celebrant:
Father, help us to understand that things are not always what we think
they are. Help us to find the deepest part of ourselves and then open
our hearts to others.

Celebrant:
We have the talent, the knowledge, and the good intentions to build
up the earth. Too often our lack of self confidence defeats us before
we begin. Let us pray for the courage to believe in ourselves so that
we can proceed with spirit and imagination.

Leader:
That we do not become so anxious to make changes in social structures
that we will not forget that justice is first a giving of ourselves, let us
pray to the Lord.

2.
That we do not value ourselves in terms of our financial worth and forget
the spirit which breathes among us, giving us life, let us pray to the Lord.

3.
For those men and women who struggle in order that the poor will have
a say in the political order which regulates their lives, let us pray to the
Lord.

4.
For those artists and scientists who labor to invent new processes of
human experience, let us pray to the Lord.

5.
That we who are the Church on earth may never be content to condemn
evil, but be willing to place our resources and ourselves at the service of
humanity, let us pray to the Lord.

Celebrant:
Father, teach us how to bring forth justice on earth without great shout-
ing and making noise. Teach us to look a disfigured man in the face before
we tell others to do the same. Father, teach us to love.

Second Sunday in Ordinary Time, page 92

ASH WEDNESDAY

Celebrant:
In fear, but also in hope, we come together with ashes on our heads.
The planet is dying in our hands; men turn to each other for food and
strength only to be shoved away. Each day we deal in death, yet pretend
that we are good guys. Let us take forty days to look hard at our so-
called goodness and see what it covers up. Then, we will join together
in taking up the cross of living in the world as it is, for there is only
one earth, and, as far as we know, only one human race.

Leader:
That as Roman Catholics we might start using our hands, feet, money,
time, and energy for the good of the poor, let us pray to the
Lord.

2.
That citizens everywhere will realize that care for their neighbor consists
in more than the mere giving of money, let us pray to the
Lord.

3.
For the needy, that they will not have to remain despondent and alone,
let us pray to the Lord.

4.
For all of us here that we will be honest enough to admit what we are
selfish about, and what we can do to remedy our lack of love, let us
pray to the Lord.

5.
For those who share Christ's charity toward sinners, let us pray to the
Lord.

Celebrant:
Lord, the ashes are our pledge to take up the cross of life. We came
from the earth and we'll go back to it. In the meantime, beginning
these forty days, we'll try to live here and make it a better home for
everybody. Through Christ our Lord.

FIRST SUNDAY OF LENT

Celebrant:
My brothers and sisters: We are the people of God's new covenant:
not by any merit of our own, but by the Father's gift to us. Therefore,
as we begin this Lent, we ask for the grace to turn from our sins to
faith in Christ's Gospel:

Leader:
For Christians everywhere: throughout Lent we will strive to listen
to every word that comes from the mouth of God. We pray to the Lord.

2.
For the world and all who live in it: may our efforts to live in peace
with one another help to make these days the truly "acceptable time"
of God's salvation. We pray to the Lord.

3.
For all who have turned away from God or who have grown careless
in their faith: may Lent be their time of new beginnings, awakened
faith, renewed friendship with God and neighbor. We pray to the Lord.

4.
For ourselves: may we reject sin with all our hearts and learn again
to live as Christ has taught us. We pray to the Lord.

5.
That we learn the humility to tell each other our needs, particularly our
need for each other. We pray to the Lord.

Celebrant:
Father in heaven,
with confidence we ask your help
to grow in holiness during Lent.
May we experience in our lives
the grace of your enduring love.
We ask this through Christ our Lord.

SECOND SUNDAY OF LENT

Celebrant:
The vision has been given to us, and the time to speak is now.
Let us pray for eloquence to fill the ears of men;
let us pray for love with which to fill their hearts.

Leader:
For the leaders of our Church, that they may love and guide us
as Jesus would, let us pray to the Lord.

2.
For law-makers, pilgrims, and prophets, that their lives may bear
witness to Christ, and that their works may do him honor, we
pray to the Lord.

3.
For those who share closely in our lives, that their love may be
like a warm tent, and transform us into images of the Father,
we pray to the Lord.

4.
For those we have rejected, deliberately or without thinking,
that the love of Jesus will heal their wounds and lead us to
reconciliation, let us pray to the Lord.

5.
That those who fear the sight of God may find his love written
in the faces of men, we pray to the Lord.

Celebrant:
God our Father, we thank you for the life and the work of Jesus
your Son. Grant us the vision and the courage to become part of
his kingdom. We ask this through the same Christ our Lord.

Celebrant:
Without the crucifixion there would have been no resurrection.
We who want to share in Christ's resurrection must first share in
the crucifixion.

Leader:
That we may take up Christ's cross and follow wherever he may lead,
let us pray to the Lord.

2.
That in our daily suffering, stress, worries and hardships we recognize
and accept our own crucifixion with Christ, let us pray to the Lord.

3.
That we see in Christ the power to save us and the wisdom to lead
us to heaven, let us pray to the Lord.

4.
That all laws and commandments be obeyed only with the love of
God and neighbor demanded by the two great commandments,
let us pray to the Lord.

5.
That each one of us be a temple of the Holy Spirit and a house of
prayer, let us pray to the Lord.

Celebrant:
Heavenly Father, accept our sacrifices in union with those of your
crucified Son, that we too may be raised up with him.

FOURTH SUNDAY OF LENT

Celebrant:
Let us pray that we may be awake when Jesus comes to heal us.

Leader:
That we recognize him in the words of Scripture, we pray to the Lord.

2.
That we recognize him in the living word of the Church, we pray to the Lord.

3.
That we recognize him in our neighbors' need for help, we pray to the Lord.

4.
That we recognize him in their cry for justice, we pray to the Lord.

5.
That we recognize him in suffering, we pray to the Lord.

Celebrant:
Lord Jesus, let us recognize you in this breaking of bread, that we may be prepared to share with you in the banquet of eternal life, where you live forever and ever.

FIFTH SUNDAY OF LENT

Celebrant:
Our lives are full of major and minor hardships, crises, decisions. We are confused and discouraged when innocent people suffer and the wicked seem to thrive. We stand helpless when those we love are taken from us in death, making us wonder anew about the meaning of life. Let us ask Christ for a spirit of joy and courage in the face of our daily trials.

Leader:
That the members of families may support each other in happy times and sad, and encourage each other in doing good, let us pray to the Lord.

2.
That widows and widowers and all who have lost their loved ones may be consoled by God's promise of new and everlasting life after death, let us pray to the Lord.

3.
That those who are weak, afraid, undecided, surrounded by the bad example of others, may draw strength from the Lord so that they not yield to temptation, let us pray to the Lord.

4.
That those who live simple and good lives may know that they are loved by the Father, even though their goodness be unrecognized and unrewarded here and now, let us pray to the Lord.

5.
That those who have gone before us in death may share in the glory of Christ as children of the resurrection, let us pray to the Lord.

Celebrant:
Father, our lives are in your hands. Turn our hearts toward you in loving confidence, and as we speak our needs to you, show us once more that you are the God of the living.

PASSION SUNDAY

Celebrant:
Confessing that Jesus is Lord, and marvelling that he became one of us
and died so that we could live, we pray to his Father with confidence.

Leader:
We pray for the whole of Christ's Church, with its pope, bishops and
pastors and all its people, that Jesus' cross may bring us to true repentance, and may teach us to proclaim his word faithfully. For this we
pray to the Lord.

2.
For those who do not believe, that we who know Jesus as Lord and Savior
may be a living sign of the love God has shown for us in his Son, we pray
to the Lord.

3.
For those who are powerful in this world, that they may seek the peace
and welfare of all for whom Jesus died, we pray to the Lord.

4.
For all who mourn over the death of those who were close, or over losses
and failures which seem to destroy their lives, or over the absurdity of
their lives, that they may know Jesus as their brother and share his triumph,
we pray to the Lord.

5.
For those whose ideals are high and whose hope is strong, that they may
persevere like Jesus to the end, we pray to the Lord.

Celebrant:
Lord, we thank you for the compassion which led your Son to come to
our aid, even though he knew he must pay for it with his life. And we
ask that we may share his compassion for our brothers and sisters, for
whom he died: in Jesus' name and for his sake.

HOLY THURSDAY

Celebrant:
We give ourselves to God by giving ourselves to others; to wash the feet of others is to wash the feet of Christ.

Leader:
That we not fail to see Lazarus waiting at our door, let us pray to the Lord.

2.
That we give what we have, namely, ourselves, in the service of our neighbor, let us pray to the Lord.

3.
That by our love, our care and concern, we humbly wash the feet of others in the many ways each of us has, let us pray to the Lord.

4.
That we be washed entirely clean by our participation in the celebration of the resurrection, let us pray to the Lord.

5.
That on our trip through the wilderness of this life to the Promised Land of heaven the eucharist be the food to strengthen and sustain us, let us pray to the Lord.

Celebrant:
Father, as we eat and drink the body and blood of your Son, given for us on the cross, help us in turn to give ourselves to you by giving ourselves to others.

EASTER SUNDAY

Celebrant:
Jesus was dead and was laid in the ground. But we know that he
has broken the power of death, and so we pray for the Life of the
world.

Leader:
For the Church of Christ, that we may have a living faith in his
resurrection, we pray to the Lord.

2.
For the newly baptized, that they may be faithful to Christ, we pray
to the Lord.

3.
For all who are returning to Christ in repentance at this Eastertime:
for the courage to live a new life, we pray to the Lord.

4.
For those who are discouraged or are in despair, that the risen Lord
may revive their hope, we pray to the Lord.

5.
For those whom we have known and who have followed Jesus into
death, that they may share with him in resurrection, we pray to the
Lord.

Celebrant:
Lord Jesus, by your death and resurrection you have shattered the
chains of death and trampled upon the powers of hell; we ask you
to grant us a share in your triumph that we may live with you forever
and ever.

SECOND SUNDAY OF EASTER

Celebrant:
Often we pray to God by asking him for things we want like good health and success in our work. Today we will praise him as he reveals himself in people. We praise God for himself; we beg him to keep us fixed on life, open to change, new ideas and the continuing splendor of creation.

Leader:
For men and women of the Church who choose to live with the poor and deprived, seeking no praise, no material wealth, that they will continue to bless us with their gentle, self-effacing lives, let us pray to the Lord.

2.
For all in disgrace with fortune and men's eyes for preaching the universal love of Christ, let us pray to the Lord.

3.
For the elderly who try to keep young in heart and show a loving interest in their children and grandchildren, let us pray to the Lord.

4.
That all men rejoice in the spirit which makes them one, let us pray to the Lord.

5.
For the bold ambitious ones among us who listen to children's complaints and old men's dreams, let us pray to the Lord.

Celebrant:
Father, we spend our lives wanting to be accepted by people we think are better than ourselves. We run away from your all-consuming love which blesses and sustains. Drive from us our need to be well thought of, for having you, Father, we are free and at peace.

THIRD SUNDAY OF EASTER

Celebrant:
Peter tells the crowd: out of ignorance you put to death the Author of life. Let us pray that *we* recognize Christ in others, that *we* always bring life, not death, to others.

Leader:
That in order to reach out Christ, we also reach out to others, let us pray to the Lord.

2.
That in order to share our food with Christ, we share our food with others, let us pray to the Lord.

3.
That in seeing the wounds of others, we see the wounds in the hands and feet of Christ, let us pray to the Lord.

4.
That we experience the joy and wonder of the presence of Christ as we recognize him in others, let us pray to the Lord.

5.
That our minds be open to the understanding of the Scriptures, let us pray to the Lord.

Celebrant:
Heavenly Father, help us be witnesses by our lives to the real presence of Christ in our world, the Christ who died for our sins and was raised from the dead for our salvation. We ask this through Christ our Lord.

FOURTH SUNDAY OF EASTER

Celebrant:
The name of Jesus is power and life.
The shepherd, Jesus, is strength and protection.
The risen Jesus is Spirit and Truth.
Through this Jesus, let us pray.

Leader:
That we may always name Jesus as Lord of our lives, we pray.

2.
That Jesus, who knows us and calls us by name, may nourish us
and call us to life, we pray.

3.
That the loving dominion of Jesus over his Church may always
be recognized in the name, "Christian," which marks his true
followers, we pray.

4.
That the sweet smell of spring may turn our minds to thoughts
of peace and life, planting and laughter, we pray.

5.
That Jesus' call may echo clearly through the pastures of the
flock that he calls; and that the idolatries of our lives may not
deafen us to the sound of his voice, we pray.

Celebrant:
Father, your name is holy,
your son is Lord,
your Spirit is life.
Shepherd us through the valley of darkness
into the kingdom of light
where you live forever and ever.

FIFTH SUNDAY OF EASTER

Celebrant:
In this assembly of God's people, as our lives are joined in serving him,
so let our hearts unite in presenting our needs before him.

Leader:
That the Spirit working in and through this parish community may
show to all that God is alive in us, let us pray.

2.
That the newly baptized may always remain rooted in Christ, called
and challenged by his Word, let us pray.

3.
That our love for those who suffer—the sick, the oppressed, the
mentally and emotionally disturbed, the poor, the hungry, the
homeless—may be real and active, let us pray.

4.
That believers who are persecuted for their faith may find their
strength in the life of Christ the Vine, let us pray.

5.
That our eyes and hearts and minds may be open to recognize our
God in unlikely faces and unexpected places, let us pray.

Celebrant:
Father, hear our prayer and increase the fruitfulness of our lives,
for it is to your glory that we have been grafted as branches onto
Christ, your Son and our Lord.

SIXTH SUNDAY OF EASTER

Celebrant:
In joyful celebration, we have commemorated the great gift of our salvation. Filled with Easter hope, let us ask God to release in us the power of the resurrection.

Leader:
That unity and charity may flower within the Church
as striking signs of the Lord's presence in our midst, we pray.

2.
That the community of the Church
may increasingly manifest
the self-giving love of Christ, we pray.

3.
That we might respect and support the work of the Spirit
wherever it is found, we pray.

4.
That we might reach out to those who are separated from us
by barriers of race, creed, or other differences,
to share with them our joy and hope, we pray.

5.
That we might grow steadily in our capacity to hear and respond
to the Word of God, we pray.

Celebrant:
Father, increase in us openness to the presence and power of the Spirit in our lives. May we so live that the Word of life may be visible for all to see.

ASCENSION

Celebrant:
Today we celebrate the exaltation of the Lord Jesus Christ.
Today we confess that all power and authority are his, and that
he lives and makes intercession for us. We gather in his name and
offer our prayers to the Father through him.

Leader:
That throughout the world the Church may witness, in the power
of the Spirit and with the perseverance of faith, to the victory of
Christ, we pray to the Lord.

2.
That the eyes of our hearts may be enlightened, so we may perceive
and hold fast to the mystery of God's love revealed in Christ, we
pray to the Lord.

3.
That through the faithful ministry of believers, the Holy Spirit,
the promise of the Father, may come upon all flesh, we pray to
the Lord.

4.
That all who are under alien power, the power of pride or resentment,
the power of hatred or fear, may be liberated to the freedom of the
living God, we pray to the Lord.

5.
That those who have died in Christ may live with him in the Kingdom
of the Father, we pray to the Lord.

Celebrant:
O Lord our God, you lead us gently to put our hope in the reality
of things our eyes of flesh do not see. Give us, we pray, eyes of love
to perceive that this Lord Jesus, who has ascended beyond our
physical sight, truly lives in our midst by the Spirit he has poured
out upon us. We make our prayer in Jesus' name.

SEVENTH SUNDAY OF EASTER

Celebrant:
Happiness and suffering are two ideas which seem opposed to each other.
Yet St. Paul, reflecting the teachings of the Sermon on the Mount, assures
us of happiness when we suffer with Christ.

Leader:
That we may accept our daily hardships and suffering
as a means of union with Christ, let us pray to the Lord.

2.
That we be happy when insulted for our faith
so God's spirit may rest on us, let us pray to the Lord.

3.
That we never be embarrassed or ashamed
for living our faith fully in every situation, let us pray to the Lord.

4.
That we devote ourselves to constant prayer
as did Mary and the apostles after Christ's ascension,
let us pray to the Lord.

5.
That we rest secure in the knowledge that Christ has entrusted us
to the care of his heavenly Father, let us pray to the Lord.

Celebrant:
Father, guard us and watch over us and give us the courage to bear
with joy our daily suffering and afflictions. We ask this through
Christ our Lord.

PENTECOST

Celebrant:
Our Easter festival concludes with today's celebration.
Through our prayer, let us entrust our lives to the Lord.

Leader:
That others may understand what we say
and not simply hear our words, we pray.

2.
That the wonders of God's deeds, and the splendors of his works,
may be praised in every language and by every tongue, we pray.

3.
That as we all experience the love of God for us here on earth,
we may be united by his love in the Kingdom of heaven, we pray.

4.
That the bond of the Spirit
may reconcile all divisions,
soothe all pain, and heal all wounds,
we pray.

5.
That travelers, students, and honeymooners
may successfully complete their pilgrimages
and be filled with the Spirit in whom all things begin
and end, we pray.

Celebrant:
Father, fill us with your Spirit as you fill us with your life.
Give us breath to praise you to the ends of the earth.
Help us to grant forgiveness, as you have forgiven our sins.
And be with us through Christ our Lord.

TRINITY SUNDAY

Celebrant:
Our God is a God of mystery living in "unapproachable light," and yet
the Lord of history who has come to live among us. We praise him now
as he has revealed himself to us: the all-powerful Father, the suffering
Servant, the Spirit of love in our midst. We ask that his presence in our
world may become more real through the lives of all who claim to believe
in him. And so we pray.

Leader:
For the entire Church of God: may laws, prestige, and protocol never be
allowed to obscure the compassionate kindness of the God whose name
we bear, whose love we proclaim. We pray to the Lord.

2.
For leaders of government: may they resist the temptation to dominate
others and allow all their people to work out their own lives in the happiness and security of a world at peace. We pray to the Lord.

3.
For courts of law, law enforcement officers, and prison officials: may
they use their power and influence to insure the triumph of dignity
over despair, understanding over punishment, and forgiveness over ven-
geance. We pray to the Lord.

4.
For the members of the entertainment world: may their celebration
of life's joy bring us happiness and their sensitivity toward its mystery
help us grow. We pray to the Lord.

5.
For teachers, parents, priests, religious, and all entrusted with the
education of the young: may their example of love help children grow
in love for God and all his creation. We pray to the Lord.

Celebrant:
Lord God,
we do not worship you as a cosmic riddle,
but as you have made yourself known to us:
Father, Son, and Spirit, a God of compassion and love,
a God who lives in us and through us.
May our ready kindness to those whose lives we touch
remind the world of your love for all creation,
of your closeness to all that is human.

CORPUS CHRISTI

Celebrant:
My brothers and sisters, there is one sacrifice pleasing to God:
that of his Son, Jesus Christ. By our prayers we unite ourselves to
the eucharistic prayer of the one high priest, Jesus the Lord.

Leader:
That this community and every community of God's people may
celebrate with joy and hope the mystery of our faith, we pray to
the Lord.

2.
That those who share in the body of Christ and drink the cup of
the covenant may be liberated from every dead work to serve the
living God, we pray to the Lord.

3.
That we who receive the body of Christ in the eucharist may be
mindful of the needs of Christ's body, the Church, especially in
its suffering members, let us pray to the Lord.

4.
That the summer may be passed in safety, and may be a
time of personal and family renewal, let us pray to the Lord.

5.
That those who have died in Christ may enter with him into their
eternal inheritance, let us pray to the Lord.

Celebrant:
O Lord our God, we confess that in Christ the fullness of your glory
has been revealed. May your Spirit empower us to live as faithful
members of Christ's body and to extend his salvation to all the
world. For we make our prayer through Jesus Christ our Lord.

Sacred Heart, page 29

SECOND SUNDAY IN ORDINARY TIME

Celebrant:
In the midst of our celebration of life pray with me for the help of
God, our Father, who affirms us and awaits our reconciliation with
all his creation.

Leader:
For Baptist, Episcopal, Lutheran, Methodist, Roman Catholic and all
denominational churches who worship in the name of Jesus Christ, that
they will openly reaffirm their brotherhood, respect each other's individuality, and find strength and compassion as sons of the same Father,
let us pray to the Lord.

2.
For our brothers, the Jews, who are a special sign of your presence
among us, let us pray to the Lord.

3.
For all who preach or speak in the name of the Lord, that their insights will be accurate, their words Christian, and their spirits alive,
let us pray to the Lord.

4.
For the men, women, and children of the world whose only fullness is
the feeling of emptiness, that a church will find them and bring them
the wine of Cana, let us pray to the Lord.

5.
For all who fear self-discipline, that the Spirit may lead them gently
into that control of themselves which makes them capable of accomplishing what they truly want, let us pray to the Lord.

Celebrant:
Help us, O Lord, to recognize our common heritage from your creation
so that we may be open and loving to each other and to all living things,
through Christ our Lord.

THIRD SUNDAY IN ORDINARY TIME

Celebrant:
We believe that Jesus is Son of God, and we ask him to lead us into his Kingdom.

Leader:
For those who are resisting God's call to repentance, to ministry, to service, or to holiness, that God may remove their defense and leave them open to his love, we pray to the Lord.

2.
For the President and the Congress, that they may find ways of working together for peace and justice in our nation and in the world, we pray to the Lord.

3.
For those who are responding to God's call, whether tentatively or wholeheartedly, that he may lead them forward with deep inward joy, we pray to the Lord.

4.
For families that are in trouble, where love is gone or is unable to make itself felt, that Christ may bring them peace, we pray to the Lord.

5.
For those who cannot get jobs or keep them, for drifters and migrants, for those who are uprooted by their work, that they may find peace in the Lord, we pray to the Lord.

Celebrant:
We thank you, Father, for the message and life of your Son, and ask that his message lead us to imitate his life, through Christ our Lord.

FOURTH SUNDAY IN ORDINARY TIME

Celebrant:
God in his love for us has given us Christ, the great prophet of all time, to teach the truth necessary for our salvation. The wise will listen.

Leader:
That our ears, opened in baptism, will always be open to hear the beautiful teaching of Christ, let us pray to the Lord.

2.
That we never be guilty of stoning the prophets, as Christ charged, but listen humbly to God's revelation, let us pray to the Lord.

3.
That God continue to raise up prophets for our time to lead us on the right path, let us pray to the Lord.

4.
That by being open to the Holy Spirit we may be filled with the Word of God, let us pray to the Lord.

5.
That we, by our lives, carry on the prophetic work of Jesus and bring the good news to mankind, let us pray to the Lord.

Celebrant:
Father, keep us clear of false prophets, abounding on all sides today. Help us accept your revelation, given through your true prophets today as in ancient times.

FIFTH SUNDAY IN ORDINARY TIME

Celebrant:
Let us open our hearts in prayer to our Father, who has shown his power to heal through his Son Jesus.

Leader:
For the sick among us, for those with cataracts or bursitis, with tumors or heart trouble or hepatitis, with fevers or headaches or any ailments, that we may feel the gentle healing power of Jesus' touch, we pray to the Lord.

2.
For those among us whose hearts are sick, who are possessed by fear or discouragement, by confusion or grief, that Jesus may cast out these demons by his word of power, we pray to the Lord.

3.
For those among us whose souls are sick, who are entangled in selfish pride, in lust, in laziness, in greed for power, in hatred, in self-sufficiency, that we may be liberated from our sin, we pray to the Lord.

4.
For those among us who are called to administer God's healing, for doctors and nurses, for the ministers of Christ's Church, for parents and friends, that we may know the power of healing which Christ puts in our hands and in our voices, we pray to the Lord.

5.
For those who have gone before us in death, that they may know the refreshment of Christ's peace, we pray to the Lord.

Celebrant:
God our Father, we know that all health and wholeness comes from you, and ask you to heal our sicknesses, our sins, and our frailty through Christ our Lord.

SIXTH SUNDAY IN ORDINARY TIME

Celebrant:
As Jesus calmed the fears of his friends, we ask him to speak his words of peace to a fearful world.

Leader:
For the overseers of Christ's Church, and for all who fear that the Church has lost its way, that they may experience the sure presence of Christ, we pray to the Lord.

2.
For the leaders of all nations who live in constant fear of one another, that they may find ways to replace this with a spirit of confidence and respect, we pray to the Lord.

3.
For all of us who live in apprehension of those who differ in age or race or politics, that we may come to know each other and live together, we pray to the Lord.

4.
For all who fear themselves, who are caught in addiction to alcohol or drugs, who cannot understand the workings of their minds and feelings, who cannot grope out of their selfishness, that they may help and support one another in their need, we pray to the Lord.

5.
For those who are about to die, that in their fear they may also know love and trust, we pray to the Lord.

Celebrant:
Lord Jesus, we believe that you are present among us as we call upon your name, and we ask you to make yourself known to us in the breaking of the bread.

SEVENTH SUNDAY IN ORDINARY TIME

Celebrant:
Aware that we may ask the Father anything in the name of Christ
and he will hear us, let us on this day of joy, of promise and of
commission place our needs before Him.

Leader:
That the Church may never lose her fervor and enthusiasm in
proclaiming the Gospel of Christ through gentle word and
compassionate deeds, let us pray to the Lord.

2.
That our vision and prayer may enlighten those in position of
power to seek justice through the equitable distribution of the
world's goods and true peace among those who share them, let
us pray to the Lord.

3.
That we may be strengthened in our faith and hope by knowing
that Jesus our Savior constantly intercedes on our behalf before
the Father, let us pray to the Lord.

4.
Knowing that we are a missionary people, may we never fail to
minister to the needs of the broken, lonely, imprisoned and sick,
let us pray to the Lord.

5.
That united through this Eucharist, we may one day share the
fullness of life with Christ and with all our departed brothers
and sisters, let us pray to the Lord.

Celebrant:
Almighty God, you have allowed us to call you Father and to
share in the richness of your life; look graciously upon our
requests and grant them if it be your will through your Son,
Jesus Christ, who as our Lord and Savior intercedes for us his
church who reigns with you and the Holy Spirit, now and
forever.

EIGHTH SUNDAY IN ORDINARY TIME

Celebrant:
Our Christianity must not be merely applied to our lives as a patch on a cloak. Our lives must be totally in Christ.

Leader:
That every thought, word and action of ours be entirely in accord with the will of our heavenly Father, let us pray to the Lord.

2.
That we who are made new in baptism remain constantly new and filled with the newness of Christ's life, let us pray to the Lord.

3.
That in our new life we see all things under the aspect of eternity, that our minds be on heavenly things, let us pray to the Lord.

4.
That we always be glad to have Christ with us, let us pray to the Lord.

5.
That we always live as members of God's family, brothers of Christ and true sons of the Father, let us pray to the Lord.

Celebrant:
Father, keep us always entirely united with you, one with you, so that we may be ever ready for heaven.

NINTH SUNDAY IN ORDINARY TIME

Celebrant:
Let us open our hearts to our Father and ask him to strengthen us
in his service.

Leader:
For those who are afflicted, like St. Paul, that they may not be
crushed; for the perplexed that they not despair; for the persecuted
that they be not forsaken; and for those struck down that they be
not destroyed, we pray to the Lord.

2.
That we may grow to enjoy and keep Sunday as a day of rest,
refreshment, and rejoicing we pray to the Lord.

3.
For those of us who try to observe the law only from a sense of
discipline and not out of love, and also for those who do not seek
to strengthen love with discipline, we pray to the Lord.

4.
For our families and our whole parish, that we will live together
with the honesty and love of Jesus, we pray to the Lord.

5.
For the old and the lonely of our city, that they may find friends,
we pray to the Lord.

Celebrant:
Lord Jesus, you found the meaning of the Law in how it fulfils
human needs. Give us the freedom to see one another's needs and
so to fulfill your law. We ask this in your name and for your sake.

TENTH SUNDAY IN ORDINARY TIME

Celebrant:
The Lord's coming is as certain as the dawn to those who call on him
with humble hearts. Let us speak to him with faith in his promises.

Leader:
For the Church, that its liturgy may be a worthy sacrifice of praise
and not an empty ritual, and that those who lead the community
in worship may be people of true and deep prayer, let us pray.

2.
For people who are considered outcasts of society, that we may be
slow to judge their sin and quick to admit our own, let us pray.

3.
For elderly people, especially those who are chronically ill, that they
may draw strength from their long lives of faith in God, let us pray.

4.
For those whose faith has not yet been tested, that they may not
waver, and for those who are struggling through the dark hours of
faith, that the presence of the Lord may dawn for them soon, let
us pray

5.
For ourselves, that we may avoid self-righteousness in our lives of
service, and formalism in our lives of prayer, let us pray.

Celebrant:
Father, make us ready to follow wherever you lead. Teach us to divest
our lives of all pretense, and to come before you as we are, weak and
susceptible to sin, but open to your healing mercy.

ELEVENTH SUNDAY IN ORDINARY TIME

Celebrant:
If God's love for man is so boundless that he allowed his son to die for sinners, then we who have been reconciled through the sacraments should join confidently in prayer to him.

Leader:
For the Church, that its ministry of peace and healing be communicated to all men, let us pray to the Lord.

2.
For the governments of the world, that their leaders will join the poor and the outcast to work for a more Christian society, let us pray to the Lord.

3.
For all who fear uncertainty, that they will risk the unknown on Jesus' behalf to find a path to salvation, let us pray to the Lord.

4.
For the suffering, the prophets of the Kingdom, that they will find peace in the promise of eternal life, let us pray to the Lord.

5.
That our friends or others who are longing or struggling to regain their faith may be able to hear the powerful words of the Gospel, let us pray to the Lord.

Celebrant:
Lord, by resurrecting your Son from the dead you have shown us the power of your word, the power to transform suffering, uncertainty, and death, the fears of all humanity, into everlasting life. Give us this day the strength to boldly walk in the steps of Jesus so that we may find the peace of your Kingdom. We ask this through Christ our Lord.

TWELFTH SUNDAY IN ORDINARY TIME

Celebrant:
Christ was rejected by the establishment of his day, by the civil and religious authorities. We who are rejected identify with Christ.

Leader:
That the many rejections we suffer in our lives may not discourage us but turn us to Christ, the one who does not reject us, let us pray to the Lord.

2.
That those who feel a loss of self-identity will find themselves as brothers and sisters in Christ, let us pray to the Lord.

3.
For the outcasts, the refugees and the political prisoners of the world, let us pray to the Lord.

4.
That we see the image and likeness of God in other people, whether they be Jew or Greek, slave or free, male or female, let us pray to the Lord.

5.
That in taking up our cross each day with Christ we will lose our life so that we may save it, let us pray to the Lord.

Celebrant:
Father, we know that you have created us out of your love. Help us to know you better, for the more we know you the more we know ourselves.

THIRTEENTH SUNDAY IN ORDINARY TIME

Celebrant:
Christ made himself poor that we might be made rich by his poverty.
We pray that we may discern what our true riches are and that we
may share with others as Christ shared with us.

Leader:
That in the deadness of our lives we let God take us by the hand
and bring us to life, let us pray to the Lord.

2.
That the song in our hearts and on our lips at this Mass be not a dirge
for our dead souls but a joyous song of thanks for God's life in us,
let us pray to the Lord.

3.
That in touching the hem of Christ's garment through the sacraments,
prayer, and Scripture, we find ourselves healed of our spiritual ills,
let us pray to the Lord.

4.
That we, made in the image of God's own nature, may rejoice that
Christ has conquered death, let us pray to the Lord.

5.
That we share our life and love with those who have not come to the
knowledge of Christ, let us pray to the Lord.

Celebrant:
Heavenly Father, who does not rejoice in the destruction of the living,
keep us safe from the envy of the devil, for only he and his way can
cause death in our hearts. We ask this through Christ our Lord.

FOURTEENTH SUNDAY IN ORDINARY TIME

Celebrant:
Brothers and sisters:
Called by Christ to be prophets, we acknowledge the weakness of our
faith, not with despair, but with confidence in our Father's love. Let us
place our needs before him, sure of his faith in us:

Leader:
For the Church, its leaders and people: may we have the courage to
speak and struggle against all that would destroy human dignity. We
pray to the Lord.

2.
For the prophets who challenge government: may men of power heed
their call to serve in honesty and peace. We pray to the Lord.

3.
For the prophets in our midst who care for the oppressed: may their
love grow strong and their work continue in the face of rejection and
hate. We pray to the Lord.

4.
For the gentle prophets whose gift is art: may we learn to hear their
song of life's beauty and pain. We pray to the Lord.

5.
For our own community: may we be a prophetic sign of Christ's presence:
serving, healing, giving in love. We pray to the Lord.

Celebrant:
Father,
in our weakness your power grows strong,
through each other you touch us with life.
Look on our needs spoken and silent,
and work within us the wonders of your love.
We ask this through Christ our Lord.

FIFTEENTH SUNDAY IN ORDINARY TIME

Celebrant:
Blessed be the God and Father of our Lord Jesus Christ, who has blessed us in Christ and given us every good gift: let us make our petitions known to him with confidence.

Leader:
For those who preach the Gospel, that they may make their message believable by their own poverty and simplicity and authority, we pray to the Lord.

2.
For those in high places, that they may not try to silence the prophets, we pray to the Lord.

3.
For the Jewish people, who were first to hope for the Messiah, that together we may live for the praise of God's glory, we pray to the Lord.

4.
For those who are suffering from ulcers and arthritis and all other sickness of body and mind, that they may hear Christ's healing word, we pray to the Lord.

5.
For picnickers and swimmers and waterskiers and gardeners and builders of sand castles, that their pleasure may bring joy to others, we pray to the Lord.

Celebrant:
Hear our petitions, Father, and grant them through Christ our Lord.

SIXTEENTH SUNDAY IN ORDINARY TIME

Celebrant:
God has taught us, the book of Wisdom relates, that the virtuous man is kind to his fellowman. We will pray that our hearts be open to the word of the Spirit and bear fruit in kindness.

Leader:
That we reflect the kindness and compassion of Christ in all our contacts with our fellow man, let us pray to the Lord.

2.
That courtesy, a sign of our love, be always evident in our dealings with both friends and strangers, let us pray to the Lord.

3.
That the good seed of wisdom which the Spirit sows in our hearts not be choked off by the details and worries of our daily living, let us pray to the Lord.

4.
That we be sensitive to the feelings, needs and weaknesses of others, in whom we see Christ himself, let us pray to the Lord.

5.
That we never reject anyone by our hardness of heart, but always be a refuge for the lonely, the outcast, the timid, the alien, the underprivileged and the derelicts of society, let us pray to the Lord.

Celebrant:
Father, most just and lenient toward us, help us truly to pray with the Spirit, for then we will pray with love for you and for all your people.

SEVENTEENTH SUNDAY IN ORDINARY TIME

Celebrant:
Christ had compassion on the multitude and in his mercy satisfied their
hunger. We pray that we be aware of the needs of our neighbor and do
our best to take care of them.

Leader:
That we give ourselves in friendship to those who are lonely, shunned,
unlikeable, and yearning for human companionship and love, let us
pray to the Lord.

2.
That we see wastefulness as a sin against the bountiful providence of
our heavenly Father, let us pray to the Lord.

3.
That we, like the prophet Elisha, so trust the Lord that we give
everything we have, insufficient though it seem, so that all will
be satisfied, let us pray to the Lord.

4.
That each one of us personally feed the hungry, for, as St. Augustine
warns, if we do not feed those dying of hunger we are killing them,
let us pray to the Lord.

5.
That through this eucharistic gathering we ready ourselves for the
eternal wedding banquet of heaven, let us pray to the Lord.

Celebrant:
God and Father of all, who works through and in all, help us to see
that when we give all we have and are, there is enough for everyone.
We ask this through Christ our Lord.

EIGHTEENTH SUNDAY IN ORDINARY TIME

Celebrant:
God alone can satisfy the needs of our hearts, and so we turn to him in faithful prayer.

Leader:
For bishops and priests, that they may be strengthened in faith and be more effective in sharing with us the Word of Christ and the Bread of Life, we pray to the Lord.

2.
For the President, the Congress, and the courts, that they may be able to restore a sense of purpose to our nation, we pray to the Lord.

3.
For all who are suffering from boredom or a sense of futility, that they may find satisfaction in helping others, we pray to the Lord.

4.
For alcholics and drug addicts and all who are emotionally crippled, that they will find help, we pray to the Lord.

5.
For little children and for retired people, that they will be happy in their freedom, we pray to the Lord.

Celebrant:
Lord Jesus, we believe that you are the true Bread that comes down from heaven; strengthen our faith and feed us with your Flesh, that we may have life in you forever and ever.

NINETEENTH SUNDAY IN ORDINARY TIME

Celebrant:
Christ is the Bread of Life who satisfies our hungers for all eternity. Starvation of our spirit will result if we fail to be nourished by this living Bread.

Leader:
That we may work together to bring Christ, our daily Bread, to all people of the world, let us pray to the Lord.

2.
For all who have left the community of Christ's faithful, that they may return to his supper table, let us pray to the Lord.

3.
That as Elijah was strengthened by food from heaven and walked to the mountain of God, may we find strength in the eucharist for our pilgrimage to heaven, let us pray to the Lord.

4.
That the eucharist, sacrament of love, rid our hearts of all bitterness, harsh words, slander and malice of every kind, let us pray to the Lord.

5.
That as Christ gave himself as an offering to God, a gift of pleasing fragrance, we too give ourselves wholeheartedly to God and our fellowmen, let us pray to the Lord.

Celebrant:
Heavenly Father, who sent your Son to give us life, keep us close to him so that we may arrive at the heavenly banquet with our nuptial robes spotless.

TWENTIETH SUNDAY IN ORDINARY TIME

Celebrant:
The Lord gathers men from all nations to witness to his glory. We here today are called to enter the assembly of men who have found the God of love. Face to face with our narrow selves and our own deep needs, we ask help for our lives.

Leader:
That we will include in our prayers and love those people we call our opponents. We pray to the Lord.

2.
That when living seems harsh, we will encourage one another to wait for the peaceful fruit. We pray to the Lord.

3.
That we will do all we can to hasten healing rather than increase lameness in the misfits and the disgraced. We pray to the Lord.

4.
That Christ will teach us to have true compassion for the drunks, the panhandlers, and people who walk down the street talking to themselves. We pray to the Lord.

5.
That the world's affluent recognize their duty to share their own with those who have no bread. We pray to the Lord.

Celebrant:
Father, our prayers gather together all our brethren, known and unrecognized, in the glory of the God of love. We will learn to reverence each man's struggle to grow and each man's pain in that struggle, as all creation with groaning and struggling moves toward God.

TWENTY—FIRST SUNDAY IN ORDINARY TIME

Celebrant:
In a world which measures value by power and possession, to whom shall
we go if we would learn the meaning of life?   Let us turn to the Lord who
bids us give of self and open ourselves to his presence in our prayer.

Leader:
For growth in willingness to give of ourselves for the benefit of others:
let us pray to the Lord.

2.
For married couples, that their love teach others the beauty of self-less
love: let us pray to the Lord.

3.
For all the world's forgotten, that someone speak to them the healing
word of life: let us pray to the Lord.

4.
For the Church's growth in faith and love, that she may dare to become
all that Christ calls her to be: let us pray to the Lord.

5.
For those in summer programs of community service, that their work be
growth and healing for themselves and those they serve: let us pray to the
Lord.

Celebrant:
Father,
see in your people the image of that Son
who came not to be served but to serve.
Open our ears to hear his word of life,
and open our hearts to live it!
We ask this through Christ our Lord.

TWENTY—SECOND SUNDAY IN ORDINARY TIME

Celebrant:
The scriptures we have shared today have a disturbing challenge to
a society that strives for conformity. We are reminded again that
God has called us in Christ to be different, to be Christ-like, and
this call demands nothing less than the total gift of ourselves. Let
us pray, brothers and sisters, for the faith to understand this challenge
and the courage to meet it.

Leader:
For all who form the holy Church of God: may we not pattern
ourselves on the greed and self-seeking of worldly values, but on the
generosity and selfless love of Christ. We pray to the Lord.

2.
For all whose dedication to the Word of God brings them insult and
persecution: may the example of Christ and our prayerful support
keep them true to the faith they share with us. We pray to the Lord.

3.
For those who search for a love that demands nothing of themselves:
may the example of Christians be an inspiration to them to open
themselves to the risk of sharing love. We pray to the Lord.

4.
For workers the world over: may they look beyond material reward
to see their work as the expression of a God-given personality and
their gift to the family of man. We pray to the Lord.

5.
For all who are travelling this [Labor Day] weekend: may they enjoy
the company of their family and friends and return to their homes
in safety. We pray to the Lord.

Celebrant:
Father, see our human weakness that drives us to enrich ourselves
without a thought for others. But see, too, our faith in Christ
and our desire to live as he taught us in the Gospel. Help us grow
into people who can love as he loved: freely sharing with others
the gifts of personality and skill you have given us. We ask this
through Christ, our brother and our Lord.

TWENTY–THIRD SUNDAY IN ORDINARY TIME

Celebrant:
Christ has done everything well. He therefore is our perfect model for all our intentions and actions.

Leader:
That our ears, opened in baptism, ever be open to the wisdom of the Father given to us by Jesus Christ, let us pray to the Lord.

2.
That by our lives we speak plainly of the love that the Father has for us, let us pray to the Lord.

3.
That we never discriminate against the poor, the mentally ill, the disfigured, the racially different, the culturally deprived, let us pray to the Lord.

4.
That we may learn to follow the way of Christ in his voluntary poverty and thus be rich in faith, let us pray to the Lord.

5.
That we learn to have only one true ambition in life, to be saints, let us pray to the Lord.

Celebrant:
Heavenly Father, Christ emptied himself and became poor that we might become rich in faith. Help us to empty ourselves of earthly ambitions and honors that we may be rich in your love.

TWENTY–FOURTH SUNDAY IN ORDINARY TIME

Celebrant:
The Word of God in today's scripture has set before us the radical call to discipleship. Let us now call upon that Lord who alone can accomplish in us the conversion to his will.

Leader:
That this congregation and every congregation of God's people may faithfully follow the Lord who has passed through death to new life, we pray.

2.
That the scandal of suffering may not become a stumbling block to believers, but a challenge to transform all things in Christ, we pray.

3.
That the sick and the aged, who experience the cross in an acute way, may also experience more strongly the consoling power of God, we pray.

4.
That the faith we profess may be manifest in the deeds we perform in Christ's name, we pray.

5.
That the joyful celebration of this eucharist enable us to pass from deadly pride to new life in the Spirit, we pray.

Celebrant.
Almighty and ever-living God, we praise you for the wonders you work in the lives of men and women. Give us a purified vision that we may understand more deeply. Give us a renewed purpose that we may follow more ardently your Son and our Lord, Jesus Christ.

TWENTY–FIFTH SUNDAY IN ORDINARY TIME

Celebrant:
The ways of advancement in our world are well known.
Instead, let us turn to the Kingdom, and pray for its
growth in our hearts.

Leader:
That social programs of power and dominance
may yield to social concerns of mutual help and respect,
we pray.

2.
That greatness be measured by service
and that service be the fruit of our love, we pray.

3.
That our enthusiasm for the Kingdom be as contagious
as a child's enthusiasm for play, we pray.

4.
That as children in the Kingdom,
we may discover and nourish our capacity for growth,
we pray.

5.
That we may make room for joys and sorrows
while we await the final coming of the Kingdom,
we pray.

Celebrant:
Father, we praise you for the presence of your Kingdom.
Help us welcome your Kingdom in its many comings,
and witness to it by words and deeds of love.
We ask you this through Christ our Lord.

TWENTY–SIXTH SUNDAY IN ORDINARY TIME

Celebrant:
Christ tells us to cut off, to remove from ourselves, anything that prevents us from entering the Kingdom of heaven. Let us pray that we have the wisdom and the courage to do just that.

Leader:
That we may turn off the TV when the time should be spent in prayer, spiritual reading, or in work which would benefit others, let us pray to the Lord.

2.
That we give away any possession or material good to which we are more attached than to our faith, let us pray to the Lord.

3.
That we overcome all habits of life which impede our progress to the heavenly Kingdom, let us pray to the Lord.

4.
That we amputate from our lives any idea, attitude, tendency, ambition or desire which would separate us eternally from our heavenly Father, let us pray to the Lord.

Celebrant:
Heavenly Father, help us to detach ourselves from anything that may keep us from union with you. Free us from an excessive greed for material possessions so that we may be unburdened on our pilgrimage to an eternity in your presence.

TWENTY–SEVENTH SUNDAY IN ORDINARY TIME

Celebrant:
Each day we receive the breath of life. Each day the
Spirit molds us in the pattern of Christ. Let us praise
God's creative love as we pray.

Leader:
That the Church may walk with sure steps in the path of Christ who
leads us to holiness, let us pray.

2.
That all nations may work to re-create our earth in the image and
likeness of God's original handiwork, let us pray.

3.
That men and women may rejoice in the image of God they find in
each other, and reject the stereotypes which bind and blind them,
let us pray.

4.
That we may learn to open our hands in thanksgiving for God's earth,
and not grasp it out of greed and violence, let us pray.

5.
That the married couples of our parish may find life and growth in
their call to be faithful, let us pray.

6.
That we may offer Christian love and support to those who
are divorced or separated, or whose marriages are troubled, let us pray.

Celebrant:
Lord God, your Son passed over from death to life, the
first-fruits of the new creation. He goes before us to
lead us into glory. Hear the prayers we offer in his name,
now and forever.

TWENTY—EIGHTH SUNDAY IN ORDINARY TIME

Celebrant:
My brothers and sisters, the Word of God which we have heard is
living and active. It penetrates to the recesses of human hearts
and makes manifest the values and hopes they entertain. Let us
conform our ways to those of God's wisdom as we pray.

Leader:
For the pastors of God's people, that they do not compromise
the Gospel's demands, but proclaim that salvation is from the Lord
alone, we pray.

2.
For the leaders of nations, that they not be deaf to the cries of
God's poor, but be attentive to the needs of the sick, the homeless,
the unemployed, we pray.

3.
For teachers and counselors, for writers and artists, that they may
bring to expression that wisdom which truly nourishes the
human spirit, we pray.

4.
For all of us who celebrate this eucharist, that we may follow
the Lord with undivided heart, we pray.

5.
For those who have died, that they may rejoice forever at wisdom's
everlasting feast, we pray.

Celebrant:
Lord our God, you teach us to put our trust in you alone. When the
way seems difficult, help us to remember that with you all things
are possible. We make our prayer through him who is your wisdom
and power, Jesus Christ our Lord.

TWENTY—NINTH SUNDAY IN ORDINARY TIME

Celebrant:
It is easier to be concerned with unimportant things,
than with the things which matter most.
Let us pray for Christian lives that matter.

Leader:
That we may seek the good of all,
and not advantage over others, we pray.

2.
That we may learn to place the service of others
ahead of our own exaltation, we pray.

3.
That the instructions of Christ
may take root in our hearts, we pray.

4.
That hardship or persecution may shape us as Christ,
not drive us to despair, we pray.

5.
That all who die
may die in Christ,
and not in defeat, we pray.

Celebrant:
Father, we thank you for the gift of your Son;
may we learn to follow his example
and become signs of his teachings
both now and forever.

THIRTIETH SUNDAY IN ORDINARY TIME

Celebrant:
It was through his faith that the blind man was healed. We pray for a strong and firm faith so that we may be healed of all our spiritual ills.

Leader:
That all who believe in Christ may be of one heart and soul, working together to cure the sickness of mankind, let us pray to the Lord.

2.
For all non-believers that they may find in Christ the love and peace for which every human heart yearns, let us pray to the Lord.

3.
For all who are faltering in their faith or who are tempted to abandon their faith, let us pray to the Lord.

4.
That our faith enable us to see Christ in the people we want to ignore, bypass, disdain or despise, let us pray to the Lord.

5.
That our holy lives, our concern for others, our consecration in the truth, be the means of bringing faith in Christ to others, let us pray to the Lord.

Celebrant:
Heavenly Father, grant to us, begotten by you in faith, a faith so intense and total that it guide us absolutely and surely to our eternal home with you.

THIRTY—FIRST SUNDAY IN ORDINARY TIME

Celebrant:
Hear O Israel!
Hear *(name of parish)*!
The Lord our God is Lord alone.
Let us pray that we may learn to serve the Lord
as true disciples.

Leader:
That our service be true prayer
and not mere words, we pray.

2.
That our service be true love
and not merely lovely, we pray.

3.
That our service give witness to God
and not to ourselves, we pray.

4.
That we may learn how to meet the needs
of the whole community, and not simply
our own, we pray.

5.
That the totality of our service
may begin to reflect the totality
of God's outpoured love, we pray.

Celebrant:
Father in heaven,
help us to hear that you are Lord alone.
Help us to be only your disciples
both now and forever.

THIRTY–SECOND SUNDAY IN ORDINARY TIME

Celebrant:
My brothers and sisters, the Word of God teaches us that we are members of Christ's body, sharing a common life. Let us present our petitions before the Lord, allowing the concerns of each to become the concerns of us all.

Leader:
That the church of Christ throughout the world may faithfully preach and practice the gospel of Christ which is spirit and life, we pray to the Lord.

2.
That we, who have begun to follow Jesus, may not find the journey too demanding, but may trust in him who has the words of eternal life, we pray to the Lord.

3.
That the members of christian families may be eager to serve one another's needs in love and fidelity, we pray to the Lord.

4.
That the aged of our society may be given a place of dignity where their experience and wisdom may benefit us all, we pray to the Lord.

5.
That our sharing in this eucharist may renew our sense of oneness and enable us to respond more generously to all who call upon us in the Lord's name, we pray to the Lord.

Celebrant:
O Lord, our God, you have called us to be holy in your sight and to be witnesses of your love in our world. Transform our hearts by the power of your Holy Spirit that we may become in truth disciples of your Christ, who lives and rules forever and ever.

THIRTY–THIRD SUNDAY IN ORDINARY TIME

Celebrant:
As we are united in welcoming the message of Christ, so let us be
united in asking the Father to hear and answer our prayers.

Leader:
For all the people of God, who seek to show their love for the
Lord by keeping his commandments, we pray to the Lord.

2.
For the innocent who suffer in the cause of right, in imitation of
Christ, we pray to the Lord.

3.
For those who have given their word but have broken it, for those
who are suspicious, afraid, unable to trust the word of God or of
other people, we pray to the Lord.

4.
For those who proclaim the Good News of the Gospel in foreign
lands, we pray to the Lord.

5.
For those who have lost the physical power of speech, for those who
are psychologically unable to communicate with others, for ourselves
when we cannot find it in our hearts to speak a word of love, forgiveness,
or healing, we pray to the Lord.

Celebrant:
Lord Jesus, flood us with the knowledge that the Father loves us as
he loves you, that you live on in us, and that the Spirit of your truth
makes his home with us.

CHRIST THE KING

Celebrant:
The spirit lives as each of us lives.
He charges us with a love energy.
He tells us not to be afraid of fearful men.

Leader:
For people who dare to paint or draw or compose music that is so
unusual that it keeps us surprised and excited about life and the sources
of life, let us pray to the Lord.

2.
That inmates of our penitentiaries and houses of detention be treated
with justice and understanding, let us pray to the Lord.

3.
For Latin American peasants we label communists every time they try to
share in the profits of their work, let us pray to the Lord.

4.
For black Americans who make the white majority confront its own soul,
let us pray to the Lord.

5.
For the people who laughed at Christopher Columbus when he said the
world was round, for the people who laughed when Edison recorded
sound, and for the people who laughed at me wanting you, let us pray to
the Lord.

Celebrant:
Father, help us to open ourselves up to heaven and earth, finding
our strength in your love. Help us to let the sun shine in.

THANKSGIVING DAY

Celebrant:
To give thanks, sisters and brothers, is to bless. It is to place all things, to see all things where they really are, in the context of the living God. So to give thanks is to see how far we have yet to go—how many and how much to pray for—until our life reflects his purposes.

Leader:
For the Churches' appreciation of God's gifts, that one fellowship of believers may be a true and vivid sign of thanks and praise, pray now and with perseverance.

2.
For the younger generations that will not accept old ways and values, that they may move us to repentance and renewal, pray now and with perseverance.

3.
For the nations and their leaders, that selfish sovereignties may yield to common needs and solidarity, pray now and with perseverance.

4.
For all those on the fringes of our social life—the poor and unemployed, the sick and handicapped, prisoners and the persecuted, refugees, homeless and the war-sufferers—that love of them may speed reform and change their lot, pray now and with perseverance.

5.
For those who have been good to us and for all who love their neighbors, that care for others may be a contagion in the world, pray now and with perseverance.

Celebrant:
If, in thanking you for that little justice, peace, and unity we have we consider our debt paid, we thank you not at all, O God. So let our humble thanks be joined with prayer and work until your Kingdom comes. Through Christ our Lord.

FIRST SUNDAY OF ADVENT

Celebrant:
Advent is a time of Good News, the good news that God loves us and has sent his Son to save us, the good news that Christ will come again to bring us to the kingdom of joy.

Leader:
That in Advent we increase the time spent in prayer and in meditating on the mysteries of our salvation, let us pray to the Lord.

2.
For unbelievers, that they might hear the good news of Christ's coming to save all mankind, let us pray to the Lord.

3.
That the Messiah bring his gifts of wisdom and understanding, of counsel and fortitude, of knowledge and piety to all of us in the season celebrating his coming, let us pray to the Lord.

4.
That the coming of the Prince of Peace may establish peace in our hearts, our homes and among nations, let us pray to the Lord.

5.
That we be truly repentant for our sins so that Christ's coming be not impeded, let us pray to the Lord.

Celebrant:
Heavenly Father, in your love for us you made our redemption possible. Help us to cooperate with your plan to make us whole and innocent again. We ask this through Christ our Lord.

SECOND SUNDAY OF ADVENT

Celebrant:

This week, we the Christian people look at our failings and beg the Father to help us not despair. We ground ourselves, instead, in the hope that the Lord will come to us. We create the future as we seek the face of God in his earth.

Leader:

That feeling the absence of meaning in the world, we will learn to take hold of each piece of earth, each color, each sound, each human voice, and in the mystery of created things find God, let us pray to the Lord.

2.

That in the midst of ideological wars and issue-centered arguments, we will discipline ourselves to be more aware of the human feelings involved, let us pray to the Lord.

3.

That we will accept failure as proof of our common humanity, realizing that we are not made for dreams alone, let us pray to the Lord.

4.

That we will accept Christmas as the mystery of God being present where we would least expect him, that is, poor among the poor. Let us pray to the Lord.

5.

That by obedience to the word of Christ the world will bury hatred and prejudice, let us pray to the Lord.

Celebrant:

Father, we ask you for the gift of yourself now so that we will not spend our lives searching for you in marble halls only to find you too late where you have always been, wrapped in the garments of the poor.

Celebrant:

God has promised to be in the midst of his people. For centuries we
have sought to unravel space and time, motion, fire, and earth, to know
the signs and the meaning of his presence. Let us pray that through his
gifts in creation we will be aware of him.

Leader:

For the Church, that it will stir our imagination, risk its life as Christ laid
down his freely, and make us brave, let us pray to the Lord.

2.

For those who have been newly elected to office, that their ideals and
energies will increase, not lessen, as the burden of serving the emergencies
of people and cities increase, let us pray to the Lord.

3.

For the countries of the Middle East, that their striving for independence
will raise up men and women to heal the burnt earth, let us pray to the
Lord.

4.

For those who control wealth, that their understanding of the world's needs
will grow, that they will share their good names and prestige with all who
seek a just way of life, let us pray to the Lord.

5.

For the weak in heart, that with John the Baptist they may find strength in
Jesus and his message, let us pray to the Lord.

Celebrant:

You have given to us, Father, the work of being open to new life, of creating
new forms of living for mankind. May the gift of your Son among us inspire
us to expand the consciousness of our own abilities, through the Spirit, in
Jesus Christ.

FOURTH SUNDAY OF ADVENT

Celebrant:

Today we remember our failings so that with our increased self-awareness we will grow into the fullness of Christ and all men will experience his love for them.

Leader:

That as we love Mary, who was a humble person, we may understand how people without power and countries without wealth are important, too. Let us pray to the Lord.

2.

That we will learn how to heal the divisions in our country between black and white, young and old, rich and poor, let us pray to the Lord.

3.

That as Mary hastened to help her older cousin who was in need, we will not be afraid of the sick and the old but will love them, too. Let us pray to the Lord.

4.

That pregnant women will deliver healthy babies and give them happy homes, let us pray to the Lord.

5.

For those addicted to drugs and alcohol, that their strength and cure can be found in God and his people, and that in us they will have true friends to see them through their crises, let us pray to the Lord.

Celebrant:

Father, as the mystery of the Christ Child draws near, do not forget us who need to know we are loved. Help us to remember the world is ours and the work of the world our work. Give us yourself, Father, give us the heart of Christ.

CHRISTMAS

Celebrant:

God speaks to us through the humanity of Jesus. Pray then, sisters and brothers, that, the humanity which Jesus shares with us may help us to devote ourselves to work for peace with one another and the world.

Leader:

For the Church and all the member churches, that we may with courage tear down the walls on which our human flesh is crucified, the walls that insulate us from our neighbors, let us pray to the Lord.

2.

For these United States, that we become a force for peace and freedom and equality, let us pray to the Lord.

3.

For persons without the strength and power of faith, that the Christ who is one with us may today open all men to the God who loves, let us pray to the Lord.

4.

For the integration of all colors and all classes in this community, in our neighborhoods and in our institutions, that humanity may make a step toward affirming itself in Christ, toward peace and brotherhood, let us pray to the Lord.

5.

For those whose flesh is hurting from poverty or sickness or the cruelty of others, that the word made flesh may use our ministry to give them strength and hope, let us pray to the Lord.

Celebrant:

Your Word was made flesh, our Father, to share our humanity. Hear our prayers, then, that we may not despise our brothers and sisters in Christ, the inequalities and barriers that wound and torture them. In the name of the Prince of Peace.

HOLY FAMILY

Celebrant:
As Christians, we can see the Holy Trinity as the image of community.
Made to the image and likeness of God, we are made to live in community.
God is Father of the human family.

Leader:
That we live together by taking care of each other, let us pray to
the Lord.

2.
That the nations which make up the world-wide family of God learn to
live in love and peace and mutual concern, let us pray to the Lord.

3.
That in our own immediate families we have the love to be more
sensitive to each other's weaknesses and needs, let us pray to the Lord.

4.
For parents, that they be a true moral authority in the home, and a bastion
of spiritual strength for their children, let us pray to the Lord.

5.
For children, that they may learn the obedience which Jesus Christ
practiced, let us pray to the Lord.

6.
For ourselves, as children of our heavenly Father, that we may always
show a constant care to preserve that bond of unity willed by Christ,
let us pray to the Lord.

Celebrant:
Heavenly Father, bind your people together as one, as you and Jesus and
the Spirit are one. Help us be merciful, kind, humble, meek, patient and
forgiving with each other. We ask this through Christ our Lord.

MARY, MOTHER OF GOD

Celebrant:
We search God's word to find a deeper understanding of Mary, and of
the Church. We turn now to God, asking that his word may be brought
to fullness in us by the power of the Holy Spirit.

Leader:
That in the faith and openness of Mary we may know and accomplish the
will of the Father, we pray to the Lord.

2.
That we who are the Church on earth may share the saving work of
Jesus, a work begun in Mary, we pray to the Lord.

3.
That our use of the earth, mother to our flesh, may be just and righteous
as we live and work, we pray to the Lord.

4.
That the year which we begin this day may be a season of growth, of deepening
and of hope for ourselves and for the family of mankind, we pray to the Lord.

5.
That those who bear the burden of government and authority may in this year
find direction and strength, we pray to the Lord.

Celebrant:
Lord and giver of Life, Holy Spirit: You gave Life to the world through the
virgin Mary; by that same loving power, give new life to us who are frightened,
and unready for its burdens. Let your glory be upon us this day and this year,
that the new world may come in us, through Jesus Christ our Lord

EPIPHANY

Celebrant:
God's promise is that wise men and women who seek his life shall find it.
Let us pray for the wisdom to discover the life of God among ourselves
and the generosity to share it with others.

Leader:
For those who serve the Church, our pope and the bishops, that as free
people with bold spirits they will show us the way to peace, let us pray
to the Lord.

2.
For all those in power, that they will understand that authority exists
to serve the people and not the people to serve authority, let us pray to
the Lord.

3.
For the victims of war and oppression, that they might discover the
compassion of Christ, and not seek in turn to destroy those who
have harmed them, let us pray to the Lord.

4.
For those lost in fear and loneliness, that we will go to them first before
we ask somebody else to take on the difficult job of loving our
neighbor, let us pray to the Lord.

5.
For ourselves, that by opening our hearts to one another, we will discover God's love, let us pray to the Lord.

Celebrant:
Father, on this feast of the Epiphany, we celebrate our discovery of
you among men. Help us to rediscover you again and again, for you
are the source of true peace. We ask you this in the name of our
brother, Jesus Christ.

BAPTISM OF THE LORD

Celebrant:
Jesus was at prayer when the Holy Spirit descended upon him and the
Father proclaimed Jesus as his only-begotten Son. We pray that we
who are made sons of God by baptism always remain filled with the Spirit.

Leader:
That we always be aware that we truly are the sons of God and live as
God's sons, let us pray to the Lord.

2.
That we may keep our baptismal robes spotless until we return to our
Father's home, let us pray to the Lord.

3.
For all of us, called by the Lord, that we open the eyes of the blind and
free prisoners from the dungeon, let us pray to the Lord.

4.
That in the trials and temptations of our spiritual life we remember
John's declaration that we are baptized in the Holy Spirit and in fire,
let us pray to the Lord.

5.
That by our prayer the heavens be opened and God's favor rest upon us,
let us pray to the Lord.

Celebrant:
Our Father in heaven, whose love for Christ was shown at his baptism,
give us strength to carry on Christ's work of healing all who are in the
grip of evil. We ask this through Christ our Lord.

Second Sunday in Ordinary Time, page 151

FIRST SUNDAY OF LENT

Celebrant:
Experience shows us that from time to time we must stand back, see where we are, and where we want to go. The work of finding the ultimate purpose of life is no exception. Lent is an opportunity to see if our association with man and God is adequate for finding our life's purpose.

Leader:
That in the Church we may find a place to sort out our confusion and disbelief, and to discover the faith and peace the Gospel brings, let us pray to the Lord.

2.
That those who wield political and economic power will resist the temptation to use that power to serve themselves at the expense of others, let us pray to the Lord.

3.
That those without power — the poor and the oppressed — will not yield to bitterness and violence, and with our help find within themselves self-respect that will set them free, let us pray to the Lord.

4.
That all of us will use our talents and resources for others as well as ourselves, let us pray to the Lord.

5.
That scientists and artists, journalists and broadcasters, will use their genius to help mankind, and not to destroy or abuse it, let us pray to the Lord.

Celebrant:
Father, help us to discover this Lent the wisdom to choose faith over cynicism, hope over arrogance, and love over selfishness. This is the way we confess that Jesus is the Lord.

Ash Wednesday, pages 10 and 73

Celebrant:
The land of peace and love, the Promised Land, is ours only after a long journey. Our faith in the power of God to move us along our road keeps us from being exiled. Let us pray:

Leader:
That God will support us when our faith is tested or our philosophies are inadequate for the crises we face, let us pray to the Lord.

2.
That confronted with the faith and wisdom of the nomad Abram, the nations of the Middle East will resolve their bitter struggle over the Promised Land, let us pray to the Lord.

3.
That men and women throughout the world who are kept from their families may create useful lives while keeping the hope of reunion, let us pray to the Lord.

4.
That those who bear the primary responsibility for peace in the world will work tirelessly to break the deadlock, let us pray to the Lord.

5.
That we will share our gifts of life and spirit with those suffering from mental or physical illness, or from old age, let us pray to the Lord.

Celebrant:
Father, continue to raise up among us men and women whose example will show us the power of your love and lead us to reflect the glory you have given our own lives through Jesus Christ.

THIRD SUNDAY OF LENT

Celebrant:
God has spoken to men in all ages, in ways too diverse to remember or write down. The wisdom of our fathers in faith will help us as we seek to find the newness of life which he has given us.

Leader:
For those who lead their countries, their cities, their churches, their families, that they will not think of themselves as safe from the failures that confront other men, let us pray to the Lord.

2.
For those who value only novelty and differences, that they will see in God's words to Moses the wisdom and righteousness which must be sought in tradition, let us pray to the Lord.

3.
For those who invoke God's name at their tables, their conventions, and on their coats of arms, that they will foster the kindness and mercy of God, seen in our sunsets, our bodies, our rivers, and our beaches, let us pray to the Lord.

4.
For those who are tempted to believe that a busy day of usual routine is a fair return on their talents, that they will not be content until they have found their deepest seeds and nurtured them to fruition, let us pray to the Lord.

5.
That we will give praise to the deaths as well as the births that take place every day, since everything that happens pushes us toward union with the source of love, let us pray to the Lord.

Celebrant:
Father, our search for new life is our Lenten goal. Give us your hand as we stumble, your light as we fall in the darkness, and new desire to find the life you foreshadowed in Jesus, your Son.

FOURTH SUNDAY OF LENT

Celebrant:
When the Israelites worked the land God gave them and no longer needed manna from the skies for food, they began to experience the freedom God wants for his people. We must work toward the freedom that God wishes us to have in our own lives, so we pray:

Leader:
That our Church leaders will encourage us and help us to break the physical and spiritual bonds which keep us from reconciling all things in Christ, let us pray to the Lord.

2.
That the major world powers, including our own, will help the weaker nations to take their rightful places in the world community, and that we will not use them to protect our own freedom, let us pray to the Lord.

3.
That we will use our skills to break the bonds of illiteracy, hunger, unemployment, and poverty that burden nearly half the people of the world, let us pray to the Lord.

4.
That we will find ways to free our native Indian citizens from reservations that hinder their freedom and that we will help them find equality in the land that was once their own, let us pray to the Lord.

5
That our school systems, including the teachers and parents, will encourage students to develop individuality and creativity, let us pray to the Lord.

Celebrant:
Help us, Lord, to be free enough to admit sin and selfishness and to seek forgiveness. May we be bold enough to accept a share in helping men feel the healing power of the Gospel of Jesus.

FIFTH SUNDAY OF LENT

Celebrant:
For the followers of Jesus, the ability to forgive is a sign of perfection, a sign which he sought but seldom found in his own day. In our time, when men are more often condemned than forgiven, let us pray:

Leader:
That those who shout angry words at the Church, or sit in sullen silence before it, will be given a patient hearing and a loving embrace by God's spokesmen, let us pray to the Lord.

2.
That political prisoners and honest critics of our way of life will not be subjected to the mockery and injustice which was Calvary, let us pray to the Lord.

3.
That broken families, once aware of the power of love, will feel the healing power of reconciliation, let us pray to the Lord.

4.
That drivers of automobiles, when harassed by others' mistakes, will not use the wheel as a weapon for revenge, let us pray to the Lord.

5.
That people who are addicted to drugs and alcohol will not be condemned, let us pray to the Lord.

Celebrant:
Stones are cast every day in public and in private. Lord, we cry for your strength to stop us from misunderstanding our brothers and sisters. Help us remember that experience, family tradition and the pronouncements of authorities do not replace the Gospel of Jesus Christ.

PASSION SUNDAY

Celebrant:
God in Christ reconciles the world to himself. He does not hold men's
faults against them, but by true sorrow for our sins, we can become
true sons of God.

Leader:
That the Churches acknowledge that they are ambassadors of reconciliation,
let us pray to the Lord.

2.
That leaders will find their support in reconciliation, not by segregation
and hatred of minorities, let us pray to the Lord.

3.
That we will come down from the Christ of our dreams and find him
where he is crucified, where honest people are condemned as being
dangerous to the public good, let us pray to the Lord.

4.
That we will praise God in the passion and fire of our lives, let us pray
to the Lord.

5.
That we may see how the mental, emotional and physical suffering of
so many people is caused by the evil of their fellow men, let us pray
to the Lord.

Celebrant:
Heavenly Father, help us put our bodies, our lives, on the line for the
sake of the neighbor in need, not for our own power and glory. Help
us to know, as Jesus did, that the only power we have against evil is
the power of our love.

Celebrant:
Jesus alone is our high priest, yet we are all priests to each other. With him we teach, heal, and lead our bodies, our minds, our earth to the kingdom of the Father.

Leader:
That the people of our neighborhoods and villages and cities will find the strength in themselves to seek the answers to dope, mugging, suicide and alcoholism, let us pray to the Lord.

2.
For all who give daily bread in welfare lines and at the altar that they will forgive daily trespasses, let us pray to the Lord.

3.
That there will someday be a table at which everyone can eat; where there are no poor and everyone is loved, let us pray to the Lord.

4.
That those who think of the Body of Christ in terms of faith alone will see Jesus in the bodies mutilated from our wars, in the punctured veins of the dope addict, in the swollen bellies of half the world, let us pray to the Lord.

5.
That the food of the eucharistic meal will become a sign of unity and love for all men, let us pray to the Lord.

Celebrant:
Father, when we eat the bread and drink the cup we proclaim the death of the Lord. We ask that we may also forgive the sins of our brothers and lay down our lives for them in memory of Jesus.

EASTER SUNDAY

Celebrant:
God's love for us has been revealed to us by his Son,
and poured into our hearts by his Spirit.
It is God's own presence which is the pledge of our hope. Let us pray.

Leader:
Father, through your Son, you have revealed to us the depths
of your wisdom and the fullness of your commandments.
Teach us to delight in the truth he came to bring, we pray.

2.
Spirit, giver of life, you are the pledge of God's great goodness to us.
Teach us to walk with joy in the way of your commands, we pray.

3.
Lord, help the people you have chosen
never to falter in hope, we pray.

4.
That the baptism which we have received
may open us to the fullness of God's life,
and release his creative, loving power through us,
we pray.

5.
Lord, your gift is fellowship with you in joy.
May our lives be an effective sign of the hope
and peace you give to those who love you, we pray.

Celebrant:
God of mercy, by your presence with us,
guide our steps along the way of truth and life.
Be light to our eyes and joy to our hearts,
that we may rejoice without ceasing
in your grace to us,
and may serve you with perfect devotion.

SECOND SUNDAY OF EASTER

Celebrant:
In Christ God has made a new covenant with us and has chosen us as his
people, so we pray to him with confidence.

Leader:
For the pope, the patriarch of Constantinople, the archbishop of
Canterbury, and all the leaders of the churches, that they may seek
communion with each other through greater faithfulness to the Gospel,
we pray to the Lord.

2.
For those of our church who never take part in the sacraments, that we
may become an ever more honest and generous community, which will
draw them back by our love, we pray to the Lord.

3.
For the poor, the lonely, the fearful, the oppressed, that our sharing in
the sacrament of the Lord may make us more sensitive to their needs,
we pray to the Lord.

4.
For those who feel lost in our liturgical changes that they may still find
Christ in or in spite of our celebration, we pray to the Lord.

5.
For people who are happy, that they may make others happy, we pray
to the Lord.

Celebrant:
You have left us, Lord, the sacrament of your Son's body and blood as
a sign of the presence of his saving work: let this sign accomplish in us
the new life which it signifies.

Celebrant:
We were not born to worship idols. We are called to live the life of the God who dances like fire in our hearts. He embraces our miserable selves and transforms us.

Leader:
For little children who are born with enthusiasm, joy and a sense of the ridiculous before we tell them to sit still, fold their hands, keep quiet and die, let us pray to the Lord.

2.
For people who smile at everyone, say, "Yes sir, yes sir," all day long and do what they are told but who lack the courage to be a light to the world, let us pray to the Lord.

3.
For people who are afraid to grow older and fatter and balder and uglier that they may learn to realize that true life and beauty come from within, let us pray to the Lord.

4.
For those people who are still not noticed because they have not noticed themselves, let us pray to the Lord.

5.
For ourselves. We grieve for our dead. We grieve for our loss. We grieve for our emptiness, let us pray to the Lord.

Celebrant:
Father, do not abandon us with only our screams, our sinking hearts, our bombs while the demons of hate invade our dreams. God of peace, possess our hearts, for you are giver and the source of life.

FOURTH SUNDAY OF EASTER

Celebrant:
The risen Christ puts all things under his feet; privileges for the rich,
the spoils of war, and customs that repress creative energies in the name
of tradition. But Christ does not crush the fragile man; he does not
bruise the man who is afraid. Instead, he lifts us up to glory; he reveals
to us the God of love.

Leader:
For people who are hungry, that we will help them to find food, shelter,
and political systems that insist on the sharing of wealth, let us pray to
the Lord.

2.
For the unemployed, that they will find a new sense of self-respect as
well as new ways of work in a world that we neither control nor dominate
and yet continue to gauge in terms of success, let us pray to the Lord.

3.
For those people whose hearts have been stolen away by the demons of
power and greed, that they may find peace in us who see life differently,
let us pray to the Lord.

4.
For people at war, especially the wounded innocents, that they may
find peace through our efforts, let us pray to the Lord.

5.
For those who suffer most from the inequalities of our society, particularly the children, that we will weep for them and so begin to open our
hearts, let us pray to the Lord.

Celebrant:
God of peace, inspire our hearts so that we will give ourselves to one
another in the same spirit that Christ gave himself to us. Give us the
courage to go about the countryside comforting people who have lost hope
in the divided kingdoms of the earth; give us the courage to be open to your
power and your light.

FIFTH SUNDAY OF EASTER

Celebrant:
The One who makes all things new, while He was yet a little while with his disciples, gave us a new commandment, that we love one another as he has loved us. Let us pray that we may learn how to dwell in love with all of God's creation.

Leader:
That our lives may preach the Good News to this, the city [town] in which we live, let us pray to the Lord.

2.
That we might commend all our lives and works to God, trusting to his grace for their fulfillment, let us pray to the Lord.

3.
That we might stay a little while with those who simply need someone to be there, let us pray to the Lord.

4.
That our love may open a door of faith for others, let us pray to the Lord.

5.
That that same love may help to build the new Jerusalem, let us pray to the Lord.

Celebrant:
Father, you glorified Jesus our brother at a moment that seemed dark and lost to his disciples. Help us who are also his disciples to perceive the hidden tribulation of heart, to recognize the hidden brother, to discern the hidden ways of love, that we might help to build a visible city of peace.

SIXTH SUNDAY OF EASTER

Celebrant:
We live in the cities of this earth bearing the burdens of our confusion
and our wars. From every side prophets arise to tell us the meaning of our
lives. We pray that we do not lose our vision of the New Jerusalem or become deaf to the whispers of the Spirit who speaks to us in the sufferings
of men.

Leader:
That empty store fronts, holes in the asphalt, vandalized cars will tell us of
our failures in the cities of the world, let us pray to the Lord.

2.
That we will seek peace by reading the facts and searching out the issues,
rather than by avoiding them, let us pray to the Lord.

3.
That by not being afraid to listen to angry voices we will begin to hear the
sorrow of the human heart, let us pray to the Lord.

4.
That we will not see the solutions we devise for the problems of our cities
or country as monuments to our immortality, but only as steps toward
better answers, let us pray to the Lord.

5.
For the poor, that they might hear the good news of jobs, housing and
the necessities of life, let us pray to the Lord.

Celebrant:
We stand firm in the life of Christ who tells us again and again, "Do not be
afraid" as he was not afraid when he was killed in the name of the common
good. The Spirit wastes no words. Father, come to us. This will be enough.

ASCENSION

Celebrant:
Before Christ ascended to heaven, he charged his followers to preach repentance and forgiveness of sins in his name, to witness to him to the ends of the earth. Now his Spirit teaches us how to pray until the day of his return.

Leader:
That we who have been chosen by Christ, may speak of the Kingdom of God by our lives as well as by our words, let us pray to the Lord.

2.
That, when the Spirit seems silent, we might abide in the city, discharging our daily tasks and waiting in patience for the time that the Father has chosen, let us pray to the Lord.

3.
That, having received Christ's Spirit of wisdom, we may grow to a deeper knowledge, in him, of the love of the Father, let us pray to the Lord.

4.
That the eyes of our hearts might be opened not only to the hope and promise of God's power but to the needs and dreams of all those around us, let us pray to the Lord.

5.
That, secure in the knowledge that this age and all ages to come and all things are under the reign of Christ, our love and patience may extend the body of the Church which he heads, let us pray to the Lord.

Celebrant:
Father, through your great power our brother Jesus was raised from the dead, and through his Spirit you have given us hope in that same inheritance. Enlighten the eyes of our hearts that we may witness to your love until he returns in glory.

SEVENTH SUNDAY OF EASTER

Celebrant:
Christ is risen. The people of God are rising. All creation will one day be made complete and glorious. Today we celebrate God's special gift of glory. We lift up our eyes to see his glory, we open our hearts in thanksgiving for the glory which surrounds us, and we wait and pray for our own completeness in his resurrection life.

Leader:
We pray to you, Father, for those poets, musicians and teachers who uncover for us the glory with which you have filled the world — from the simple glory of plants and animals to the overwhelming mystery of just being alive. For them and all who turn us on to your glory, let us pray to the Lord.

2.
That the Church may be filled with the expectancy, the glow and excitement of what it means to be your Bride, awaiting the radically new future you are now creating for us, let us pray to the Lord.

3.
For new life in our schools, that they may become involved in our struggle for humanness as well as competence, let us pray to the Lord.

4.
For those who are waiting in desperation; for some sign that life is O.K., that people can be trusted, or for those who are just waiting without knowing why or for what, let us pray to the Lord.

5.
And for those who have seen your glory so clearly and have died sharing that vision; for Stephen, the first Christian martyr, for Abraham, Martin and John, and for all who suffer in bringing glory and honor to this planet, let us pray to the Lord.

Celebrant:
Father, you promise glory and splendor to your people. As we prepare to offer to you. our gifts of bread and wine, we offer ourselves, our families, schools and nation as well. We offer them in the bread and wine to be transformed and restored to us as living, glorious beings. Bring all things together in your glory, Lord.

PENTECOST

Celebrant:
God does not love us more than he loves the Russians or the Chinese.
Why do we build walls between ourselves and the people we call enemies?
Are we the light of the mind? Have we invented the sources of life? On
Pentecost we pray that we will be open to the life who alone sustains us
and who pushes us to that unity of love which is the revelation of God.

Leader:
For the leaders of governments that they will give us order rather than disorder, peace rather than the destruction of peoples, lands and cultures,
let us pray to the Lord.

2.
For unrepresented peoples that we will be aware of them and give them a
fair hearing, let us pray to the Lord.

3.
For the people of faith in every part of the world, and for ourselves, that
with the spirit of Christ we will work to heal our personal and our institu-
tional wounds, let us pray to the Lord.

4.
For those lacking direction in life, that through our love they will find
meaning and a vision worthy of their energies, let us pray to the Lord.

5.
For people who live in fear of public opinion, that from seeing the
spontaneity of our lives they will come to know the spirit of God in themselves, let us pray to the Lord.

Celebrant:
Father, you create us with power to move mountains. Most of us lack the
courage to move ourselves. We are afraid of becoming lights on the mountaintop because somebody might hate the light and try to put it out.
When will we die with Christ to our inhibitions and our fears so that with
Christ we can rise to new life? When, Father, will we let your Spirit live
in us?

150   *Pentecost C*

SECOND SUNDAY IN ORDINARY TIME

Celebrant:
Our individual lives depend on the lives of everyone else, particularly those workers we take for granted: miners, migrant farm laborers, factory workers. Let us pray for the silent poor who are the ground of our lives.

Leader:
For salesgirls and bus drivers, for ushers and tenant farmers and artists, for short order cooks, for street cleaners, for hospital orderlies, for doormen and bootblacks, let us pray to the Lord.

2.
For the unemployed who despair because they have no way to express their energies, no way to contribute to society or to support themselves, let us pray to the Lord.

3.
For those who live in so much self pity and self hatred that they cannot see the work to be done in their own back yards, let us pray to the Lord.

4.
For those people who take care of the elderly, the dying, and the mentally ill without seeing any improvement, let us pray to the Lord.

5.
For the courage to do the work we enjoy doing even though that work might offer little prestige and small financial reward, let us pray to the Lord.

Celebrant:
Father we did not create ourselves. We cannot sustain ourselves. But we fool ourselves into thinking that our schedules and our plans will direct the power of God in us. Help us to loosen up and let your Spirit flame out where it will. Help us to love the talents we have and not imitate those we don't have lest we block your power in us and wither like grass.

Trinity Sunday, pages 27 and 90

Corpus Christi, pages 28 and 91

Sacred Heart, page 29

THIRD SUNDAY IN ORDINARY TIME

Celebrant:
We gather together, feeling our tie with all men. We gather in your name to listen to your word and to live that word so that we can grow. We open our eyes and ears to the Spirit who keeps us together, even when we keep trying to divide the earth.

Leader:
For the Church, that we will be given sight in our blindness, let us pray to the Lord.

2.
For the authorities of the State that they will free those political captives who have offered their lives for justice's sake, let us pray to the Lord.

3.
For the minority groups in our town and state that they might get out from under our oppression, let us pray to the Lord.

4.
For leaders in the community and in the world, that they will serve us, their brothers, with love and reconciliation, let us pray to the Lord.

5.
For all who preach or speak in the name of the Lord, that their insights will be accurate, their words Christian, and their spirits alive, let us pray to the Lord.

Celebrant:
Most of all, Father, we ask that you give us strength to keep together; we need everybody we've got.

FOURTH SUNDAY IN ORDINARY TIME

Celebrant:
If mankind is to hear the good news of creation, men and women of every generation must speak with courage and love. Let us pray for the courage to brace ourselves for action in the Lord's service.

Leader:
For all who serve the Church, that they will be true prophets in their hunger for justice, let us pray to the Lord.

2.
For political leaders and men of authority, that they will have the courage to love those they serve, even when they are hated and mis-understood, let us pray to the Lord.

3.
For those subject to unjust laws and regulations, that they will have the courage to resist that authority, let us pray to the Lord.

4.
For those who see people treated with injustice and oppression, that they may love their brothers enough to speak and act against such cruel authority, let us pray to the Lord.

5.
That each of us may recognize our radical need for courage and for love and our need for one another, let us pray to the Lord.

Celebrant:
Father, we hear your word; we hear your command to preach the word. We pledge to grow in our love for one another so that we may stand before you with Jesus our brother.

FIFTH SUNDAY IN ORDINARY TIME

Celebrant:
There is no proper season for discouragement. Our old fears of the dark keep us blocked, congested, unable to move when everything we are as Man pushes us to discovery and new life. Today we look at the Christ who does not doubt the life which is given him.

Leader:
For singers, comedians, and playwrights who struggle to affirm life, often at a terrible cost to themselves, let us pray to the Lord.

2.
For scientists and inventors who labor in darkness so that the hard earth will yield its light, its energy, its healing powers, let us pray to the Lord.

3.
For those who are in prison, let us pray to the Lord.

4.
For parents of retarded children and blind children and emotionally disturbed children who must fight an uphill battle, let us pray to the Lord.

5.
For those people dying of terminal diseases who find it impossible to let out their spirits into the deep sea of the Lord's forgiveness and mercy, let us pray to the Lord.

Celebrant:
Father, we do not bow down before you like slaves. You are the light of our bodies, the breath that gives us life. We praise you by taking risks, by celebrating new discoveries and ideas, by not letting failure destroy us. Because you live, Father, we cannot die.

SIXTH SUNDAY IN ORDINARY TIME

Celebrant:
The Sermon on the Mount describes for us those states of soul which
give us access to God. We pray for the humility to open our aggressive
selves to tears, poverty, and peace, so that unburdened by external
concerns we will grow to understand the basis of life and the sources
of joy.

Leader:
For those who mourn: for widows and orphans, for people who have
tried and failed, for soldiers who return from war to find no one who
cares they went, let us pray to the Lord.

2.
That we will increasingly value people for what they are, not for what
they have and base our decisions on those values, let us pray to the Lord.

3.
That we will stop being afraid of poverty but will think about those
people who had nothing and still were happy; Francis of Assisi,
Vincent de Paul, Christ, let us pray to the Lord.

4.
That we will not be afraid to cry when we feel like crying, lest we
become unable to grieve at the death in our lives, let us pray to
the Lord.

5.
For the peacemakers the world calls cowards,for the pure of heart
the world calls simpletons, for those who hunger for justice whom
the world calls troublemakers, radicals and maniacs, let us pray to the
Lord.

Celebrant:
Father, where is the source of our energy, our creativity, our life?
Does wealth sustain us or power or prestige? We pray that you will
remember us, so that having your kingdom we will be rich and never
afraid.

SEVENTH SUNDAY IN ORDINARY TIME

Celebrant:
The battle between life and death rages in each one of us. We cannot selfishly stifle our concern for each other's lives. Today we affirm life at its deepest sources by trying to love our enemies.

Leader:
That we admit to the destructive forces in ourselves, let us pray to the Lord.

2.
That we will not passively accept as our enemies those people our government tells us are our enemies, let us pray to the Lord.

3.
That we see the destructive nature in comparing ourselves to men who have won a certain glory by using other people and by exploiting their work, let us pray to the Lord.

4.
For the apostles of non-violence in our midst, that we try to understand the enormity of their task and not expect them to be angels in order for their work to be valid, let us pray to the Lord.

5.
That in giving to others we learn to relax our souls, let us pray to the Lord.

Celebrant:
Father, you have given us a life which sustains us, continues us, pushes us to greater complexity and depth. No other person except ourselves can kill the life in us, a life which unfolds to the extent that we embrace the world even with its terrors and its ugliness. Remember us, Father, and we will suffer no harm.

EIGHTH SUNDAY IN ORDINARY TIME

Celebrant:
The world tells us to compete. We learn to gain our souls by getting ahead. The name of the game is survival. Why should we be shocked when we are at war within ourselves admitting no God into the proceedings unless he pays our taxes and our dues. We pray for the peace of Christ which cannot be gained if we do not love our enemies.

Leader:
That we admit we are often angry with ourselves and self-destructive in the way we look for attention, let us pray to the Lord.

2.
For the courage to seek peace and justice in the world, let us pray to the Lord.

3.
That we will not passively accept as enemies those people our government tells us are our enemies, let us pray to the Lord.

4.
That we will face up to the fact that Christ was executed as a public criminal and a traitor and consider the implication of his action in our lives even though we are fearful and without sufficient strength, let us pray to the Lord.

5.
That we may learn to forgive those who have hurt us and treated us unfairly, let us pray to the Lord.

Celebrant:
Father, we will hide from your face, seeking peace in things which cannot give us peace. Things like power, wealth, success. We live in constant fear of being invaded, of being destroyed, as if we were empty inside and needed filling up. You are already there, Father. Help us to unblock ourselves and feel your presence in our guts.

NINTH SUNDAY IN ORDINARY TIME

Celebrant:
Today we celebrate the greatness of the Lord, who lifts the spirits of
the fallen, loosens the tongues of those silenced by guilt, who raises
the buried, and overcomes doubt with trust. We pray for the power of
the Holy Spirit to lift up life through his Son our Lord.

Leader:
That when the world is boring and leaders are without imagination, we
may receive vision, new insights, and courage to point to the issues,
let us pray to the Lord.

2.
That when friends are uninteresting, and there is little left to say,
we may find new topics, and our conversation find new concerns,
let us pray to the Lord.

3.
That when guilt builds up like walls, the Lord will use us to break it
down with forgiveness and understanding, let us pray to the Lord.

4.
That when we have little success and little of which to boast, Christ will
give us a sense of importance by the meaning of his grace, let us
pray to the Lord.

5.
That when we are imprisoned in word and deed by forms of society
which cripple, Christ will give us clear minds and free speech to risk
new possibilities, let us pray to the Lord.

Celebrant:
Lift up life, O Lord. Strengthen and renew creation by what we are
doing, saying, building and celebrating. In the excitement and mystery
of your word we may turn aspiration into action and thoughts into
deeds which tell the world — Christ lives!

TENTH SUNDAY IN ORDINARY TIME

Celebrant:
Today we put our trust in the Lord and in the events through which he brings life. If we believe in the resurrection of Jesus then we will come to him for what we need to know and for the healing of what needs to be made well.

Leader:
That we invest our time and skills in those things in our community and world which have deep value, knowing that so often what glitters is not gold, and what is green is not always living, let us pray to the Lord.

2.
That we turn our interest and abilities to areas where there is human need, and where help can be received, let us pray to the Lord.

3.
That we find freedom in the community of the Church to express our faith and unbelief, and keep loving one another, let us pray to the Lord.

4.
That we hear the Word of the Lord in the signs and expressions of our society, let us pray to the Lord.

5.
That we have the wisdom to see the extraordinary in the ordinary times and places, and to know Christ when he is close, let us pray to the Lord.

Celebrant:
O Lord, as we recheck our list of priorities and put to the top what belongs there, help us make decisions which make living a glad thing. May our way of seeing Christ in daily events, within the limitations of our strength and circumstance, reflect a growth in optimism and hope. Through Christ, our Lord.

ELEVENTH SUNDAY IN ORDINARY TIME

Celebrant:
In this age as in the centuries preceding it, there have always been people who have courageously challenged men who challenge those ideas which restrict the freedom of the human mind. Men who love the outcasts of society will suffer condemnation. Civilization calls them mad. So it was with Jesus Christ. Socrates. Sigmund Freud. We pray for the vision to see life whole.

Leader:
That city councils will speak to the issues, listen to citizens' complaints, and become the prophets of new life, let us pray to the Lord.

2.
That people who write books and edit newspapers will give us a vision of life and our place in it, let us pray to the Lord.

3.
That those who collect bottles for recycling, and plant trees, and cover up strip mines, will show us how to care for the creation we have been given, let us pray to the Lord.

4.
That the angry will develop cool minds to put their energy to use, and that those who have no anger will open their hearts to the fires of injustice in this world, let us pray to the Lord.

5.
For the people who live in the slums of hopelessness and garbage, rats and stinking buildings, pollution and apathy, that they might feel the sunshine of a better life, let us pray to the Lord.

Celebrant:
Father, we acknowledge the truth of Christ's love in the world. Love was always the beginning and the end with him, the root of his existence, the offspring of his mind. We do not really know what love is. Our movies betray us. Our songs rarely last from one year to the next. Father, we ask you for yourself. When we know who you are we will know ourselves and know ourselves as no longer alone.

TWELFTH SUNDAY IN ORDINARY TIME

Celebrant:
We are brothers and sisters in the same Spirit who lives and breathes in each of us, the Spirit of love who pushes us to a greater involvement with him and with each other and with ourselves. We praise God who is the source of all life and love.

Leader:
For people who run away from their responsibilities, let us pray to the Lord.

2.
For communists, capitalists, pessimists, personalists, religionists, humanists and all who divide up the world, that they will confess to each other the unity of love they crave above all, let us pray to the Lord.

3.
For those people who know everybody's problems and nobody's genius, let us pray to the Lord.

4.
For soldiers who don't get mail, children who flunk, showgirls who grow old, for all who suffer, that they will know there is no suffering unnoticed by God, let us pray to the Lord.

5.
For all Americans, that major world tragedies will not blind them to the little daily murders of denial, rejection and defamation, let us pray to the Lord.

Celebrant:
Father, help us allow the spirit you have given to each of us transform our lives and our world. He lights the path. Give us the strength to follow him through Christ our Lord.

THIRTEENTH SUNDAY IN ORDINARY TIME

Celebrant:
As disciples of Christ we are possessed by the Spirit who transforms us into lovers as we re-create the earth. We pray for the courage to listen to those voices which affirm life and bless the rocks, the water, the sun, and the moon.

Leader:
For people who are afraid of happiness, let us pray to the Lord.

2.
For all of us, that we will keep love of life and our sense of humor, let us pray to the Lord.

3.
For the pure of heart who see the good in every man, let us pray to the Lord.

4.
For men and women who put their hope in the hands of dictatorial leaders because they feel no strength in themselves, let us pray to the Lord.

5.
For migrant workers, that seeing the earth put forth new life they will rise up and overcome the forces of death, let us pray to the Lord.

Celebrant:
Father, help us love in Christ who rises up to reveal the Spirit in each of us. We live and breathe because he is the God of love.

FOURTEENTH SUNDAY IN ORDINARY TIME

Celebrant:
The Gospel tells us we are a new creation and appoints us as lambs among wolves. Could we, peaceful Christians that we think we are, consider ourselves successful people if we didn't have our armies, our dollars, or our American citizenship? Where does the strength of the saint come from? What is the success of Christ?

Leader:
For a world governed by the Consent of the Governed and recognizing that all men are created equal, that they are endowed by their Creator with certain inalienable Rights, that among these are Life, Liberty and the Pursuit of Happiness. Let us pray to the Lord.

2.
For all whom we weep for but do not want as next door neighbors. We pray to the Lord.

3.
That we treat with true compassion those people who are forced to live on welfare. We pray to the Lord.

4.
For our brothers and sisters arrested without provocation and jailed without bail, that they will find peace for their souls. We pray to the Lord.

5.
For people whose jobs enslave them, waste their energies and send them home a little more dead than the day before. We pray to the Lord.

Celebrant:
Father, we put our hope in our ability to defend the rights of the poor, the homeless, the put upon. We want to be known as the saviors of the oppressed, forgetting you alone are the source of freedom. We open ourselves to the Spirit who is wind and fire and the victory of life and we praise your name.

FIFTEENTH SUNDAY IN ORDINARY TIME

Celebrant:
We acknowledge that the commandment God has given us is not hard
to remember; it is as close to us as our hearts and our mouths. We ask
for each other's support in carrying it out.

Leader:
For the victims of violence and injustice, that we will raise ourselves
up to defend them. We pray to the Lord.

2.
For those priests and levites among us who ignore the needs of broken
men as they hasten about their sacred functions. We pray to the Lord.

3.
For the good Samaritans of our day, who belong to other churches, but
who serve their brothers in simplicity, that we will bless them in their
work. We pray to the Lord.

4.
For ourselves and all men and women of faith, that we will come to know
God and love him with all our mind and soul. We pray to the Lord.

Celebrant:
Father, in Christ your Son who is one of us we see   what your love is;
we see who you are. We ask you to so transform the lives of us who use
your name, that by seeing us men will believe in your love and will praise
your glory.

SIXTEENTH SUNDAY IN ORDINARY TIME

Celebrant:
As the Lord dined with Abraham and as Jesus dined with Martha, even
though they could not see his glory, we know that the Lord is among us
at this sacred meal; and so we turn to him in faithful prayer.

Leader:
For those who, like Sarah and Martha, are overwhelmed with the work
of serving others, that they may also find time to sit at the Lord's feet
and listen to him, we pray to the Lord.

2.
For women who have learned like Mary that their place is not only in the
kitchen, that hearing the Word of God they may use their liberty to put
it into practice, we pray to the Lord.

3.
For bellhops and maitre d's, for hotdog vendors and stewardesses, for all
whose work is hospitality, that they find in their work the satisfaction
of serving Christ's brothers and sisters, we pray to the Lord.

4.
For those who have no meal to eat and for those who eat alone, that they
may find means to gain their food and friends to share it with, we pray to
the Lord.

5.
For those who are entrusted with preaching and teaching Christ's Word,
that they may understand his message and speak it compellingly as he did,
we pray to the Lord.

Celebrant:
God our Father, we have listened to your Word and have shared it;
now we pray that the Sacrament which we are sharing may strengthen
us to accomplish what you have said. We ask this in Jesus' name

SEVENTEENTH SUNDAY IN ORDINARY TIME

Celebrant:

At times it is hard for us to think that prayer makes any difference, and yet, Abraham bargains with God and Jesus speaks of God as a friend and a father who listens and responds to our petitions. This is the faith that not only leads us to pray, but to discover the response of all creation to our openness before it.

Leader:

For those children who hear our sermons about God, who memorize our answers and our meaning of life and do not feel our warmth, let us pray to the Lord.

2.

For those men and women in prison who pray for our downfall as they struggle to live in a cage and do not feel our warmth, let us pray to the Lord.

3.

For those people who are embarrassed at being alive, who hate their bodies and speak in a hush and do not feel our warmth, let us pray to the Lord.

4.

For people who flunk out of school, get fired from their jobs, cry in their sleep, and do not feel our warmth, let us pray to the Lord.

5.

For a new style of life, that we and all Christians can be known by the warmth of our caring, let us pray to the Lord.

Celebrant:

All powerful, ever living God, you are not ashamed to be called our Father, and we are not ashamed to come before you as children and ask for the things we need. The gift we seek above all, however, is not a thing but a person, the gift of your Holy Spirit, whom you have promised to give to all who ask and who will transform our minds and hearts in the image of your son, Jesus Christ. To him be the power and the glory now and forever!

EIGHTEENTH SUNDAY IN ORDINARY TIME

Celebrant:
In baptism we put on a new self which opens us to the freedom of man and the glory of the God of love. We pray that we will keep ourselves open to life. We pray for the wisdom to let the Spirit work in us.

Leader:
That we will be grateful enough for the profits we make from other's labor to share the profits with the laborers, especially our South American and African brothers. We pray to the Lord.

2.
That we will accept the healing gift of rest and stop pretending we can sustain our own spirits. We pray to the Lord.

3.
For people who pick themselves off the floor of repeated failures and rejoin life with the passion of a clown and the energy of mountain climbers. We pray to the Lord.

4.
That we will stand before the anxiety, envy, covetousness, and contention in the world and in ourselves with humility and so worship God. We pray to the Lord.

5.
That we will reverence the mystery of other people's lives and of our own life when we use words like Negro, middle-class, culturally-deprived, and PhD. We pray to the Lord.

Celebrant:
Father, we are tempted to turn to the old idols of Me First and Get Rich Quick forgetting we have a new self in Christ who is fully open to God and man. We will put to death the falseness that keeps us from our interior freedom. Possessed by the Spirit of Christ we will come to know the heart of God.

NINETEENTH SUNDAY IN ORDINARY TIME

Celebrant:
In every age God calls men and women to be his people. His call is never to security and ease, but to openness and risk. This was his call to Abraham, to Moses, to Jesus. This is his call to us: to risk our good name, to rise above prejudices, to join one another in building a world of justice, a union of peace. With confidence we pray.

Leader:
That we find through our openness to the God of love the courage to struggle against injustices, regardless of the consequences. Let us pray to the Lord.

2.
That we use what power we have for the enrichment of life and not be afraid to admit our errors. Let us pray to the Lord.

3.
That we who have been given much accept a Christian attitude toward the problems of the poor: one of help and understanding. Let us pray to the Lord.

4.
That we use our scientific talents to develop and preserve this earth for the enjoyment of generations to come. Let us pray to the Lord.

5.
That we learn to sacrifice our comfort, our time, ourselves, to love one another. Let us pray to the Lord.

Celebrant:
Father, in the gospel Christ tells us that the Kingdom of peace and wisdom and love is entrusted to our care. Building a just and peaceful world is a long and difficult process. Give us your life so that our faith is not a shield from life's problems but a sharing in the life of God.

TWENTIETH SUNDAY IN ORDINARY TIME

Celebrant:
The God of love is no respecter of personages. The life of each of those
whom the world calls unsuccessful and who are anonymous is dear to him.
The man in solitary confinement, the dying child, the so-called failure,
the bum; their tears flow like rivers into the heart of God. Let us pray.

Leader:
For Christians who worship Christ the King and yet look down upon
the sweaty workingman. We pray to the Lord.

2.
For Christians who honor the Immaculate Conception and know nothing
of the Mary who is the pregnant bride, the refugee, the mother present at
her son's execution. We pray to the Lord.

3.
For Christians who attend the Sermon on the Mount several times a year
but who have never quite made it to Calvary because there is blood there,
violence, and seeming defeat. We pray to the Lord.

4.
For Christians who applaud Salome the dancing girl and say nothing about
John the Baptist, who is locked in the cellar for speaking out against
established authority. We pray to the Lord.

5.
For Christians who would rather stay on the mountaintop worshipping
a transfigured divinity than go with him into the cities embracing the
blind, the deaf, and the diseased. We pray to the Lord.

Celebrant:
Father, we dream of power and wealth, removing ourselves from your
Spirit whose power is the power of love and whose wealth is the gift of
joy in all your creation. Through Christ our Lord.

TWENTY–FIRST SUNDAY IN ORDINARY TIME

Celebrant:
The conflicts of life test our faith in man and God, yet in conflict we sometimes come closest to each other. Pray to be a free people with faith in yourselves and others, patient yet willing to deal directly with all.

Leader:
For those who try to stop big wars, confront big business, and demand justice for little people, that they may show us a world that is not in a textbook, let us pray to the Lord.

2.
For judges, that they will have the faith for a just cause to rule against the power that put them in office, let us pray to the Lord.

3.
For all who have lost themselves, that they will recognize their own strength, let us pray to the Lord.

4.
For a society where we don't have to make a million dollars, run the 100 in 10 seconds, invent a laser or die, in order to be believed, let us pray to the Lord.

5.
For the "have-nots" of the world, that they will not be destroyed by the "haves" who are too selfish to share and too blinded to see, let us pray to the Lord.

Celebrant:
Lord,
We accept your Word in scriptures. Help us correct the errors in our society and proclaim the message so that our world can become one with yours through Christ our Lord.

TWENTY—SECOND SUNDAY IN ORDINARY TIME

Celebrant:
The man or woman who recognizes the Spirit is open to the forces of
human life and truly stands before the Lord. We pray now for ourselves.

Leader:
That we will always be gentle to the destitute, the aged and the lonely
and not blame them for their suffering. We pray to the Lord.

2.
That we will not look down on people with sexual identity problems
but will embrace them with the warmth they need, we pray to the Lord.

3.
That we will not waste our time and energy being impressed by those with
Rolls-Royces and world renown but will look to the needs of those in
trouble and pain, we pray to the Lord.

4.
That we will give way to angry people who tell us we are devils and pigs
as we seek the good of our brothers and sisters, we pray to the Lord.

5.
That we will always be grateful that as crippled as we are in our abilities
we are glorified in the love we bear one another, we pray to the Lord.

Celebrant:
God of Life, our brother Christ is the revelation that we will know you
when we respond to death and destruction with a merciful heart. As
the Spirit opens us to love, we take pleasure in the material world, transforming it and praising life.

TWENTY—THIRD SUNDAY IN ORDINARY TIME

Celebrant:
As we join in prayer, welcome the world into our midst and seek the wisdom that leads to the straight paths in life.

Leader:
For the world's leaders: religious, political, academic, and economic, that, as trusted guides, they will be gentle and honest with all men, let us pray to the Lord.

2.
For new strength to hate, actively hate, injustice, poverty, inequality and war, let us pray to the Lord.

3.
For the stamina to follow the Gospel of Jesus Christ, to carry our crosses faithfully when we would prefer to rest, let us pray to the Lord.

4.
For the twisted, misunderstood, tortured lives whose only direction in life seems toward death, let us pray to the Lord.

5.
For a frost that will tarnish the value of gold and put sparkle into the dullness in life, let us pray to the Lord.

Celebrant.
Father,
another summer of our life is gone. Help us renew our commitment to you, to our brothers and sisters here and to all mankind, that together we may follow the clear path your Son has given us. We ask this through Christ our Lord.

TWENTY–FOURTH SUNDAY IN ORDINARY TIME

Celebrant:
So much of life seems like a gigantic game of hide and seek. "I dare you to find me," "Why don't they notice me?" Hiding and seeking. It's so hard, and we're so afraid. Let us pray for honesty and for strength in finding ourselves.

Leader:
Lord, have mercy upon us for playing games with others, with ourselves, and with you. We pray to you, O Lord.

2.
Forgive us the ways we have of copping out on ourselves, of choosing more than our share, and messing ourselves up in the process. We pray to you, O Lord.

3.
That we may develop an eye for seeing what we are doing to ourselves and to our friends, let us pray to the Lord.

4.
That we may accept the simple fact that we are loved beyond belief and that when we tire of playing our games you are there to welcome us home, let us pray to the Lord.

5.
For the blessed relief from selfishness by staying close to Christ, let us pray to the Lord.

Celebrant:
Father, too often we have it all mixed up. We hide in so many, many places. And all the time you are seeking us and waiting for us. Help us to come out of hiding and help us on our way home, into ourselves and to you.

TWENTY–FIFTH SUNDAY IN ORDINARY TIME

Celebrant:
Brothers and sisters, God has given each of us, even the poorest, some wealth for which we are responsible—our lives, the dignity and feelings of others, our earth, this community. Let us pray that we might be faithful to this trust.

Leader:
Remembering that Christ Jesus gave himself for all, may we never try to bargain, openly or by hidden ways, for the liberty and honor of our fellow men, let us pray to the Lord.

2.
For those in authority, that they will not abuse their power or forget that it is primarily for the service of others, let us pray to the Lord.

3.
Knowing how much we have received, may we remember to thank God as well, let us pray to the Lord.

4.
And knowing how much we owe to our fellow men, may we be generous to all with whom we meet, we pray to the Lord.

5.
And that we may wisely use the things of this world, not pursuing elusive wealth of material or of opinion, let us pray to the Lord.

Celebrant:
O God, your Son gave himself so that we might give ourselves in your love. By your Spirit may we become worthy stewards of this one truth by which you would have all men saved.

TWENTY–SIXTH SUNDAY IN ORDINARY TIME

Celebrant:
Pray for those who need what we possess and for those who possess
what we need. Pray that we may not turn deaf ears to these harsh
scripture words, but that our lives and our resources may be aimed
at an end of both rich and poor—reconciled in your kingdom's equality
and solidarity.

Leader:
For the Churches and the humble signs of unity we have in our pope,
and our bishop, that we preach and live to make the human family one
in sharing everything, pray together.

2.
For those in governmental power and influence, that world and national
economies be geared to human needs rather than to greed and profit,
pray together.

3.
For cooperatives of every kind and all means of social ownership, that
we may build structures and institutions in our daily lives more friendly
to the Gospel, pray together.

4.
For community organization in city, neighborhood, and parish, that no one
among us may be in want unless we are all in want, pray together.

5.
For this congregation, that the sharing and the solidarity we here express
and celebrate may be real in all of our relations, pray together.

Celebrant:
It is not easy, God, to pray that we may bridge the great abyss between
the rich and poor. Our comfort may depend upon that great abyss. So
free us and strip us, and make our wills and action the accomplices of
your reconciling Spirit.

Celebrant:

Our world is much like the prophet Habakuk's: violence and senseless destruction seem to be the only news we hear. With the prophet we ask: Why? And God's answer to us through Jesus is the same: have faith in the vision of peace and love you see, and by your faith make that dream a reality. We gather a broken world into our thoughts as we pray:

Leader:

For all whose lives have been scarred by the violence of others, that men and women of vision will touch their lives with love and give them reason to love again. We pray to the Lord.

2.

For the young, that they will have the courage to face the world as it really is, while never losing faith in what man can be. We pray to the Lord.

3.

For those who have grown convinced of man's basic brutality, that the Spirit open their eyes to see the Christ who lives in every man. We pray to the Lord.

4.

For those who serve in public office, that they never accept as normal the violence of poverty and discrimination in our land. We pray to the Lord.

5.

For the leaders of the Church, that they continually call the Christian community to serve the needs of all the world, asking no privilege or reward in return. We pray to the Lord.

Celebrant:

God, our Father, in Christ you have shown us how to face the violence and evil that lives in our world. He experienced at first hand all that is worst in man's nature, yet died with a prayer for his killers and rose to set all men free. Keep his vision of love alive in our hearts.

TWENTY–EIGHTH SUNDAY IN ORDINARY TIME

Celebrant:
The world locks chains around men, slaves to powers both real and ima-
gined. A Christian's freedom from the enslavement of death celebrates
the freedom of life.

Leader:
For the leaders of the Church of Christ, that they will find ways of
communicating the cleansing joy of the Gospel to all men, let us pray
to the Lord.

2.
For those rulers in the world whose laws, or guns, or lies, enslave millions,
that they will be transformed by love to bring freedom to their people,
let us pray to the Lord.

3.
For plastic surgeons, psychiatrists, and all physical and psychotherapists,
that they will continue to develop their science for the benefit of all men,
let us pray to the Lord.

4.
For the sick, the sad, and the infirm, that they will find in themselves and
in us hope for new life, let us pray to the Lord.

5.
That we eagerly look for Christ's coming in the need and in the service
of our neighbors, of strangers, of all our brothers, let us pray to the Lord.

Celebrant:
Father, we ask you to look after our brothers who cannot help themselves.
Show them to us and help us in our daily lives to seek out those whose
conditions repulse us. We ask this through Christ our Lord

TWENTY—NINTH SUNDAY IN ORDINARY TIME

Celebrant:
Our prayer for one another's needs is itself an act of faith. Like Moses, we lift our arms and keep them lifted. Like the insistent widow, we do not cease to bring the needs of humanity before the living God in common prayer.

Leader:
That the Son of Man, when he comes, will find faith and freedom on earth, let us pray to the Lord.

2.
That the churches will always see faith's witness as their work, their mission, their most liberating and dynamic gift, let us pray to the Lord.

3.
That the hurts and disappointments caused by Christians will not blind men and women to the word of God, let us pray to the Lord.

4.
That believers may be free of all those interests that inhibit their love of neighbor, let us pray to the Lord.

5.
That the poor, the sick, the prisoners, and all in any way oppressed may find us free enough to be their friends, let us pray to the Lord.

Celebrant:
We take faith's vision, and all your church has meant to humankind, so much for granted, God, that we do not even understand what life would be without its presence. Hear our prayers for all of us, because all stand in need. And free us by our faith for life's new possibilities.

THIRTIETH SUNDAY IN ORDINARY TIME

Celebrant:
We who seek to serve God know that he alone is the true judge and that he listens to prayer that rises from humble hearts. Let us pray.

Leader:
May God let us see ourselves as sinners, yet know that we are loved in our frailty and that He alone is the source of righteousness, let us pray to the Lord.

2.
That our prayers and our words and our deeds may pour forth like a libation, an offering, but never as a bribe, let us pray to the Lord.

3.
May we learn from God's mercy to heed the cries of those in need, let us pray to the Lord.

4.
That we might not abandon our brothers, and when we feel abandoned by them that we will not hold this against them, let us pray to the Lord.

5.
May we be patient in prayer and in service, proclaiming the Gospel by our trust and love, let us pray to the Lord.

Celebrant:
O Father, who hears our prayers, who loves us in our littleness, may we proclaim your Son in the service of our brothers, in our fidelity to Him and to them, in eager patience for his coming and in the humility and love of his Spirit. Through Christ our Lord.

THIRTY—FIRST SUNDAY IN ORDINARY TIME

Celebrant:
God's love and sustenance of all creation theatens the attitudes we have maintained towards our neighbors and our planet. We can find beauty when we look for it. Let us pray.

Leader:
For people we have denied by not allowing them into our lives, that they have found love in someone else, let us pray to the Lord.

2.
For activists who spend lonely days fighting strip mining companies, water and air polluters, and others who ravage this world, that they will find support and strength, let us pray to the Lord.

3.
For rich men the world over that they will give of their wealth to the needy, let us pray to the Lord.

4.
For orphans and lonely children that someone will bring them love and protection, let us pray to the Lord.

5.
For the crumbling of barriers that separate Jew and Arab, Black and White, East and West, let us pray to the Lord.

Celebrant:
Lord, we pray for the strength to wash away ingrained bigotry, to be open to the needs of our neighbors. Help us see the beauty of your creation and work to develop and protect it. We ask this through Christ our Lord.

THIRTY—SECOND SUNDAY IN ORDINARY TIME

Celebrant:

We are waiting for Christ to come to us in his fulness. We still have much work in the world, building new cities, reaching the hearts of men with our love.

Leader:

For the broken hearted, especially the poor who have not caused their own suffering, let us pray to the Lord.

2.

That we may be filled with the joy of those who are open to life, who do not define the world before they make it happen, let us pray to the Lord.

3.

That we may find the happiness of Mary who recognized her strengths and her blessings, let us pray to the Lord.

4.

That we may take the risk of seeing the good in the people we share our lives with, let us pray to the Lord.

5.

That in the people we meet we may recognize Christ, let us pray to the Lord.

Celebrant:

Father we are grateful to know our failings so that we may grow in self-awareness. Give us yourself so that we may fully share in the mystery of Bethlehem.

THIRTY—THIRD SUNDAY IN ORDINARY TIME

Celebrant:
Each person here must suffer and die. No man or woman lives without fear and deprivation. Let us pray for humility to understand the radical human experience so that we do not too easily choose sides and draw up battle lines without knowing who we are.

Leader:
For the broken, disillusioned people in our lives, that we may have the courage to love them and help them, let us pray to the Lord.

2.
That we may know what it means to be a prophet, to discern the times and to speak out at the risk of being disliked, let us pray to the Lord.

3.
That we fight for peace by first making peace with ourselves, let us pray to the Lord.

4.
That with Jesus our brother we may come to know how God is more especially with the poor, the despised, and the forgotten, let us pray to the Lord.

5.
For people who are filled with hate and fear, that they might slowly be opened to the freedom and joy of faith, let us pray to the Lord.

Celebrant:
Heavenly Father, help us to see things as they really are, and to know in our hearts that Jesus is the last word in good news, and that obedience to him is the way to wholeness.

CHRIST THE KING

Celebrant:
Our Father created a Kingdom for us to inherit. We join together as hopeful heirs of that Kingdom to pray to him for our brothers and sisters throughout the world.

Leader:
For our pope, our bishop, our parish priests, and all who work to reconcile the world, let us pray to the Lord.

2.
For the great nations created through Christ and for him, that they will reconcile their differences and bring peace to the world, let us pray to the Lord.

3.
For those in prisons, who despite their faults and failing are still our brothers in the Kingdom, that Christ will bring them to paradise, let us pray to the Lord.

4.
For all who are contemptuous of Christ, that they may share the peace of his Kingdom, let us pray to the Lord.

5.
For our alienated, unemployed, titleless brothers and sisters who wonder what all this talk of a Kingdom is about, let us pray to the Lord.

Celebrant:
Father,
you have given us your first-born, in whom all life was created. Help us nurture and care for this kingdom we have, the sky, the earth, the waters, our brothers and sisters, through Christ our Lord.

Thanksgiving Day, pages 63 and 125

JOSEPH, HUSBAND OF MARY

Celebrant:
As a congregation gathered with Joseph's own humble trust and hope
in the Spirit, let us pray to the Lord.

Leader:
For a community where man may work with dignity at a trade he loves,
where he may support and shelter his family, and live to see his children
and his children's children find peace and fulfillment in this world, let us
pray to the Lord.

2.
For a Church where free men may labor as brothers, as among equals,
vibrant with the life and strength of the Kingdom begun by Christ, let
us pray to the Lord.

3.
For all who have been deprived of their fathers and their father's work,
through slavery, starvation, abandonment, and annihilation, let us pray
to the Lord.

4.
For foster parents and parents by adoption that they will find true
happiness in the mystery of parenthood they share with St. Joseph,
let us pray to the Lord.

5.
For us, that we might let in the Spirit of peace that commits us to a
new vision of man and his city, let us pray to the Lord.

Celebrant:
Father, give to all men the strength you gave Joseph to do your will
when he did not understand it. Help us trust in your word as he
trusted in your spirit and thus may we share with Christ in making the
world your Kingdom on earth.

ANNUNCIATION

Celebrant:
The will of God is in us. We have put aside blood offerings and religious wars in order to face up to our birthright and our glory which is love for the brethren.

Leader:
That as the warmth of spring brings new life to the northland, the leaders in the world will bring peace to the world, let us pray to the Lord.

2.
For winners of the Nobel Peace Prizes, and all who work to make the land more productive, let us pray to the Lord.

3.
That each of us may be as open as Mary to the will of the Spirit, let us pray to the Lord.

4.
For women, the handmaids of the Lord, that each may find fulfillment through the inspiration of the Spirit, let us pray to the Lord.

5.
That all will recognize the miracle of God in themselves and rejoice in it, let us pray to the Lord.

Celebrant:
Father, teach us to surrender to that life we did not create and cannot sustain. Draw us toward you, toward that union which is our freedom. Through Christ our Lord.

BIRTH OF JOHN THE BAPTIST

Celebrant:
We have heard that John was chosen from birth to go before the Lord to prepare his ways. We pray today especially for those whose vocations most closely resemble those of John's parents and of John himself.

Leader:
For expectant parents and parents of little children, that they will know how to love them, we pray to the Lord.

2.
For missionaries and for all who preach Christ where he is unknown, that they will be able to distinguish their own prejudices from the message of the Kingdom, we pray to the Lord.

3.
For all who preach and teach, that they will proclaim the Good News with power and authority and joy, we pray to the Lord.

4.
For nuns and monks and hermits, and especially for those whose way of life keeps them from having much to do with other humans, that they may hear the word of God in their desert as did John, we pray to the Lord.

5.
For all who are not married or are living alone, that they may be free to find ways of bringing peace and joy to others, we pray to the Lord.

Celebrant:
God our Father, your prophet John fled to the desert to know you in silence and prayer, but he also preached your Kingdom and led the multitudes to repentance. Lead your Church to a knowledge of you that is beyond shallow acquaintance, and so make us speak the message of repentance and of the Kingdom with greater effect. We ask this in Jesus' name and for his sake.

PETER AND PAUL, APOSTLES

Celebrant:
Let us pray that the Lord who called Peter and Paul to be his apostles and martyrs will revive their spirit in the world.

Leader:
That the Church of Christ will know the stability and unity which Jesus pledged by founding it on the rock which is Peter, we pray to the Lord.

2.
That we will experience Paul's zeal to spread the message of Christ, we pray to the Lord.

3.
For those who, like Peter, are in prison, that they may learn the freedom which the Gospel brings, we pray to the Lord.

4.
For those who suffer indifference, ridicule, hostility, rejection, or persecution because they are faithful to Christ, that their loyalty may be strengthened, we pray to the Lord.

5.
That the message of Christ which we have received through the apostles may make us more generous in the service of our fellow men, we pray to the Lord.

Celebrant:
Look kindly on us, God our Father, and grant us the prayers we make in Jesus' name.

PETER AND PAUL, APOSTLES

Celebrant:
Reflecting on the faith of Saints Peter and Paul, let us with confidence place our needs and the needs of this community before the Lord.

Leader:
That the Church may be healed of her divisions and factions and thus proclaim the Word of God with one heart and one voice, let us pray to the Lord.

2.
For all those whose decisions affect the lives of others, that guided by the Spirit of Christ, they may seek peace and justice by word and example, let us pray to the Lord.

3.
For all of us who have accepted the Gospel of Christ, that we might not count the cost of our discipleship but rely upon the Lord to sustain and strengthen us, let us pray to the Lord.

4.
That those who suffer for Christ and his message; for those who seek his presence and saving power, and for all who look to the Church for the healing power of Christ, that they may not be disappointed and be ever sustained by God's love, let us pray to the Lord.

5.
That we may acclaim Jesus as our Saviour and Lord through works which manifest his Spirit—compassion, forgiveness, mercy and joy,— let us pray to the Lord.

Celebrant:
Father, you have given us models of faith and courage in the lives of Peter and Paul; through their intercession hear the needs of your people and grant them through Christ our Lord.

TRANSFIGURATION

Celebrant:
As we remember Christ's appearance to his apostles in light, we pray
that his glory may still shine in the world.

Leader:
For our bishops, priests, and all who lead God's Church, that their faith
may be founded on Christ and may lead us in truth to our Father, we
pray to the Lord.

2.
For young people, for those who are trying to make sense out of life
and the world, that the message of Jesus may be spoken in a way that
has meaning for them, we pray to the Lord.

3.
For old people, for contemplatives, for the sick: may they experience
the glory of God in the face of Christ Jesus, and be witnesses to us that
there is more in life than what we have seen. For this we pray to the Lord.

4.
For busy people, who feel the urgent need to transform the world, and
who cannot now take time for reflection, that they may have a vision
of the kind of world God wants, and may find joy in the struggle to bring
it about, we pray to the Lord.

5.
We pray for those who face death, courageously or with terror, whether
their lives have been lived to the full, or been dissipated, or been scarcely
tasted, that they may share with Peter and James and John the vision of
Christ's glory, we pray to the Lord.

Celebrant:
Our Father, God, kindly give to your Church the experience of Christ's
presence and of his majesty, that we may have the strength to follow him
in his poverty, his humility, his courage, and his constancy. We ask this in
Jesus' name and for his sake.

ASSUMPTION

Celebrant:
The Lord Jesus has been raised in the flesh, and has shown that our bodies are God's creation and can live forever. Let us pray that the splendor of God's creation may be seen in us.

Leader:
For the beautiful, that they will grow more handsome with age, we pray to the Lord.

2.
For the homely, that their hearts may be beautiful enough to show through, we pray to the Lord.

3.
For the old, that we may love their mellowness and character, we pray to the Lord.

4.
For the middle-aged, that we may admire their strength and support their weariness, we pray to the Lord.

5.
For the young, that we may be tolerant of their youth, we pray to the Lord.

Celebrant:
Our Father, God, we believe that you have raised your Son Jesus from the dead and given his mother Mary a share in that resurrection. Let us also share with them in life eternal, through Christ our Lord.

ASSUMPTION

Celebrant:
Each of us, like Mary, is given a unique role in God's plan.
Let us pray for a growth of Mary's vision in our hearts.

Leader:
That the Church may proclaim God's greatness in all its words
and works, let us pray.

2.
That we may open our eyes to the hidden power of God
transforming all of creation into a sign of his glory, let us pray.

3.
That we may learn to find our joy in the great things
God does for us, let us pray.

4.
That those who have gone before us in faith may share
in Christ's victory over death, let us pray.

5.
That the victims of poverty and injustice may find comfort in
Mary's proclamation that God casts down the mighty and raises up
the lowly, let us pray.

Celebrant:
God, your goodness reaches from ages past even to this day.
Fulfill your promises to us, so that our descendants too
may praise your mercy.

ASSUMPTION

Celebrant:
Our lives and our world often seem in anguish. But our pain is the anguish of delivery, as our individual and corporate Christ-lives come to birth. We pray that we will be born again in the spirit who gives us life.

Leader:
That those who live in the wilderness of sorrow, confusion and death might trust in the God who has prepared a place for them. We pray to the Lord.

2.
For those brothers and sisters we have accused and judged. We pray to the Lord.

3.
For those who need us, that we will greet them with the joy of people grounded in life. We pray to the Lord.

4.
That we will rejoice at the growing freedom of people who were slaves and support the liberation of people who are closed in upon themselves with bitterness and fear. We pray to the Lord.

5.
That we will be open to the fulfillment of all that Christ speaks when men will be one with each other and with the God who is the source of life. We pray to the Lord.

Celebrant:
Father, we exult in you, even as we cry out in the anguish of being born again. We know that Christ triumphs over all domination and lust for power, and that we, with Mary, will rise into the victory of total self-giving.

ALL SAINTS

Celebrant:
Throughout the ages men and women have followed Jesus. We pray that we may walk in their footsteps.

Leader:
That our bishops, pastors, and teachers will show forth the spirit of the Apostles so that their message will have the power to convince those who are open, we pray to the Lord.

2.
For people who are laughed at or discriminated against or persecuted for trying to live like Christians, that they may have strength to persevere like the martyrs, we pray to the Lord.

3.
That leaders of our nation and of other nations may have the wisdom and compassion of the saints who were kings and chancellors and peacemakers, we pray to the Lord.

4.
That those who drop out of our society may have the longing for God, the gentleness and purity of the holy hermits and pilgrims who went before them, we pray to the Lord.

5.
May all of us follow with joy and simplicity the great throng of men and women who have gone before us with steady strides, or stumbling and wandering but finding their way back to the way of the Lord. For this we pray to the Lord.

Celebrant:
Lord, we thank you for this feast of all your friends, and ask that we may be in that number when the saints come marching in.

Celebrant:
If we call ourselves God's children we can expect the world to ignore us, as it refused to acknowledge his Son. Pray then for those who find no peace or recognition in this world.

Leader:
For Presidents, Kings, and Dictators, that they may find happiness being poor in spirit, let us pray to the Lord.

2.
For the strong men and bullies, that they may find happiness being gentle, let us pray to the Lord.

3.
For the selfish that they will hunger and thirst for what is right, let us pray to the Lord.

4.
For the unforgiving that they will find happiness in being merciful, let us pray to the Lord.

5.
For the judges, juries and wardens, that they will support the human side of the law, let us pray to the Lord.

Celebrant:
Lord,
it is difficult to find happiness when we are abused and persecuted. Help us face the world as your sons and daughters, accepting the bitterness, calumny, and hate of all threatened by your word through Christ our Lord.

ALL SOULS

Celebrant:
Death, proud death, has been given a death sentence by Christ's death and resurrection. We pray for all who have died to this world that they may enjoy never-ending life with our common Father.

Leader:
For family and friends who have died, that they take part in the heavenly wedding banquet where God himself will put on his apron and wait on them, let us pray to the Lord.

2.
For our parishioners, separated by death from this Christian community, that they enjoy the heavenly community of Father, Son and Holy Spirit, and the angels and saints, let us pray to the Lord.

3.
For those who through our failure to bring food and peace have died from hunger and war, let us pray to the Lord.

4.
For all who have died, that in death they pass to complete freedom, to the land where there is neither tear nor sorrow, let us pray to the Lord.

5.
For ourselves, that we see death as a sign of God's love and look forward to death with serenity and confidence, let us pray to the Lord.

Celebrant.
Father, welcome the departed into your bosom as you welcomed Lazarus who was poor. Welcome us also in our time, though we may be poor in faith, hope and love. We ask this through Christ your Son, who died that we might live.

ALL SOULS

Celebrant:
Every man is condemned to death, but by the grace of Christ's death and resurrection our seeming condemnation becomes a blessing for all eternity. We pray that we be prepared for that infinite beatitude.

Leader:
That all who have participated in the death of Jesus Christ by faith and baptism may share by death the shining splendor of his resurrection, let us pray to the Lord.

2.
That all people experiencing the solitary and single act of death be fortified by the love of Christ, the help of the Church and the concern of friends, let us pray to the Lord.

3.
That we see the call to death as a personal call from our heavenly Father to join him and his family in the marriage feast of heaven, let us pray to the Lord.

4.
That by faith our anxiety about death be transformed into happy expectation, let us pray to the Lord.

5.
For our family and friends who have died, that their deaths be a response to the love by which Christ has invited them home, let us pray to the Lord.

Celebrant:
Father, help us to grow in faith and love that we may see death as our birth in the beautiful kingdom of heaven. Prepare our hearts to accept the gift of death. Grant that the faithful departed find that fullness of peace which only you can give. We ask this through Christ our Lord.

IMMACULATE CONCEPTION

Celebrant:
Today we honor the Virgin Mary, who gave birth to God's only Son;
who heard God's word and kept it. We ask her to join in our prayers
for the needs of the world for which her Son died.

Leader:
For peace and justice among nations, we pray to the Lord.

2.
For justice for the poor and oppressed, we pray to the Lord.

3.
That Christ's Church may hear God's word and keep it, we pray to the Lord.

4.
For courage and comfort to the suffering, we pray to the Lord.

5.
For harmony and growth in our families, we pray to the Lord.

Celebrant:
We thank you, Father, for the gifts with which you prepared Mary to be
mother of your Son, and ask you to make us free like her, and open to
your word, through Christ our Lord.

IMMACULATE CONCEPTION

Celebrant:
Today we celebrate the great lady of our lives, the humble Virgin who saw life whole and loved it, giving us the freedom of a total humanity.

Leader:
That we learn the true values of sex in both the married and single life, let us pray to the Lord.

2.
That we learn to see our own authority, when we have it, as a chance to serve others and that we have the courage to question those who, having authority, do not serve, let us pray to the Lord.

3.
That as Mary was born of a people who were poor and without political power, we may learn to see beyond differences in people and love them as we love ourselves, let us pray to the Lord.

4.
That in the crippled, the imprisoned, in those who experience life as drugs and battlefields, we may learn a new understanding of God, let us pray to the Lord.

5.
That we will come to know better the free heart of the girl who gave birth in a stable, fled her country and saw her son executed as an enemy of the state, let us pray to the Lord.

Celebrant:
Father, we celebrate the woman of whom the poets sing. Give us yourself and raise us up, so that in suffering and in death we will always see your face.

IMMACULATE CONCEPTION

Celebrant:

We tell ourselves that all things are possible with God. The presence of
Mary in the Church gives us daily proof that from the beginning God
has prepared signs of his glory. With her faith let us ask for a renewal
of these signs today.

Leader:

For those whose names appear in headlines: pope, bishops, presidents,
governors, mayors, that their ideals will transcend geography, race, and
the generation gap, let us pray to the Lord.

2.

For those who haul garbage, clean our parks and streets, inhale dirt and
fumes, that their work and lives will be blessed as they help us keep the
world clean, let us pray to the Lord.

3.

For employers whose primary interest is in efficiency, self-confidence, and
good appearance, that they will also hire the ugly, create a demand for the
unwanted, and support those who are new on the job, let us pray to the
Lord.

4.

For those who are dulled by jobs or circumstances, that they will find
creative work, opportunities to move, resurrection on the day of death,
and new songs to sing, let us pray to the Lord.

5.

For those whose cupboards are bare and whose tongues are parched, that
they may find room at some table, let us pray to the Lord.

Celebrant:

God, from Mary you raised up a Savior. May Mary's song be our song
always, and may what you have done through a maiden, now be done
through us, in the name of this Savior who lives forever.

MEMORIAL DAY

Celebrant:
Memories are joyful and painful, but we cannot live without them.
Let us pray that we may never forget.

Leader:
For leaders who send young men to war,
that their judgments be sound
and their motives be pure, we pray.

2.
For soldiers who lay down their lives for others,
that the love which inspires their sacrifice
be fulfilled in the love of Christ, we pray.

3.
For soldiers who have been maimed or brutalized by war,
that our love for them may make their scars of no consequence
and make their brutality yield to the tenderness of returning love,
we pray.

4.
For those who have been left behind,
that they may live on the strength of the love that they knew,
we pray.

5.
For those who suffer most from war,
that the homeless, the orphaned, the hungry, and the innocent
may help us turn from warlike ways to pursue the potential of peace,
we pray.

Celebrant:
Father, help us never to forget that war is hell.
Help us to honor its saints, and to pray for its sinners and victims,
through the Victim for our sakes, Christ Jesus,
our Lord.

INDEPENDENCE DAY CELEBRATION

Celebrant:
On this Independence Day we know more than ever that only the truth
will make us free. Let us pray to God, the Father of truth and of freedom.

Leader:
That we may be free to change ourselves and the structures of our
society in the light of the demands of God's Kingdom, let us pray.

2.
That we may be free to place our talents and resources at the service
of those who most need them, let us pray.

3.
That we may be free to accept not only our rights but also our
responsibilities as citizens, let us pray.

4.
That we may be free to learn from the past, neither repeating our
mistakes nor rejecting our heritage, let us pray.

5.
That we may be free to shape a future of peace and justice for all,
let us pray.

Celebrant:
Our nation was conceived in risk and revolution in the struggle for
freedom. In your presence, Father, we recommit ourselves today
to that struggle. May we be as willing as our fathers and mothers of
generations ago to risk "our lives, our fortunes, our sacred honor"
so that true freedom, and not oppression, may be the hallmark of
this nation. We make this prayer through Christ our Lord.

LABOR DAY

Celebrant:
The Bible story of creation teaches that work is good but that
sin can make it a curse. Creation is the work of God; sin is
the work of man. We, the created image and likeness of God,
must work to restore the original splendor of this world, God's
handiwork.

Leader:
That love of God and neighbor be the motive of all work, both
physical and mental, let us pray to the Lord.

2.
That employers work with employees as fellow-workers, sharing
the burden of perfecting living conditions for all of God's family,
let us pray to the Lord.

3.
For employees, that they recognize the dignity in good labor,
give full value for their wages
and treat their tools and means of production as God's property,
let us pray to the Lord.

4.
For capitalists, that they see property as lent to them by God for
the benefit of all mankind, let us pray to the Lord.

5.
For members of labor unions, that they be active and responsible
in their unions, and for their leaders, that in union activities they
be guided by the virtues of St. Joseph, the worker, let us pray to the
Lord.

Celebrant:
Heavenly Father, maker of all things, help all workers, whether in
the home, school, factory, field, or elsewhere, to love each other and
therefore to work for each other in the one Body of Christ, for we
are all workers in the vineyard of the Lord.

LABOR DAY

Celebrant:
Let us join the work of our hearts and hands to that of Jesus
the carpenter, Mary the homemaker, Peter the fisherman, and Paul
the tent-maker, as we present our needs to the Father.

Leader:
For the Church, that it may not allow any other task to overshadow its
primary work, that of reconciling the world to God, let us pray.

2.
For the unemployed and for their families, let us pray.

3.
For those whose work is dull or dehumanizing, let us pray.

4.
For those who create things of beauty or of usefulness,
for those who shape meanings out of words and symbols,
for those who work to bridge gaps and heal wounds, let us pray.

5.
For those who are retired or can no longer work, that they may know that
their worth depends, not on what they do, but on who they are,
let us pray.

Celebrant:
Lord God, bless our labors with success. May all our work
contribute to the building of your Kingdom.

BAPTISM

Celebrant:
As a people reborn, let us pray for ourselves, our children,
and our world, that Christ may be our way of life.

Leader:
For all Christians, that they may be faithful to their baptismal
promises, let us pray.

2.
That all who have died with Christ,
may live so as to rise with him,
let us pray.

3.
That the parents and godparents of *N.*
may live so as to inspire him with a love
and respect of Christ, let us pray.

4.
That we may help to shield *N.*
from the influence of evil in this world,
let us pray.

5.
That our weak faith may be strengthened
to see in this watery grave the pool of everlasting life,
let us pray.

Celebrant:
Father, we thank you for the new life you bring into our community.
Renew the faith of all your people so that we may praise you and
pursue you all the days of our life.

BAPTISM

Celebrant:
Lord, you want little children to come to you,
grant that this child may show us the way.

Leader:
As this child is helpless without us,
may we learn how helpless we are without God,
we pray.

2.
As this child is curious to explore the world,
may we be curious to explore the ways of faith,
we pray.

3.
As this child will trust and be open to us,
may we learn to trust God's ways for us,
we pray.

4.
As this child cries until his physical needs are satisfied,
may we cry out to the living God until our spiritual needs are satisfied,
we pray.

5.
As this child smiles at all who take an interest in him,
may we daily exhibit the joy of those who are loved by God,
we pray.

Celebrant:
Lord, we come before you with open hands and empty hearts.
Pour the fullness of your grace into your people,
that as children we may seek and find the joys of your Kingdom.

BAPTISM

Celebrant:
What kind of community are we, that we dare initiate new members
and call them, by that fact, "Christians"? What do we really have to
share with the new members whom we welcome but our faith, our hope,
our love? We pray now for these candidates and for all our fellow humans,
that the power of the Lord's death and resurrection will give them a new
lease on life...and will open possibilities of freedom for us all.

Leader:
For the communities of faith, that we will place our lives and our possessions at the service of the human family, for the sake of justice, let us pray
to the Lord.

2.
For the unbaptized, that their faith may orient them to the living God,
and that we will unite with them as a vigorous sign of the equality to which
all of us are called, let us pray to the Lord.

3.
For these persons to be baptized this day, that we will not stifle them or
quench the spark of life they share with us, let us pray to the Lord.

4.
For ourselves, that our affirmation of the living God above all human
idols may be so strong, so purposeful, inviting such commitment, that it
lifts our hearts and the hearts of our neighbors, let us pray to the Lord.

5.
For the oppressed, the sick, and the troubled, that our belief in the Christ-
life will convert the wealthy, heal the suffering, and lead us to care for one
another, sharing our wealth and our gifts, let us pray to the Lord.

Celebrant:
The initiation we celebrate and witness, God, is more than a cleansing bath.
It is a return to the sources of life. We ask you to hasten the fulfillment of
your promises. Give us the boldness to accomplish justice, and turn our
hearts to you. Through Christ our Lord.

CONFIRMATION

Celebrant:
We are working people and we are a praying people. We become Christians by a process of initiation that begins with baptism, and continues with confirmation and the eucharist. We pray now for those to be confirmed today, and for the world which we in the Church are learning how to serve.

Leader:
For the bishops of the world and for our bishop here, that as signs of unity in all the churches they will steadfastly set their hearts on God, let us pray to the Lord.

2.
For those to be confirmed, that the second step of their initiation will confirm the direction of their lives in the footsteps of the Christ who walks as a free man among us, let us pray to the Lord.

3.
For these young men and women, that the laying on of hands will be a sign that we care for them, that we want to share our lives with them, let us pray to the Lord.

4.
For our community, as well as all the other churches, that the strengthening in fellowship we celebrate today may be more than memory, more than a half-forgotten rite, let us pray to the Lord.

5.
For all who suffer imprisonment, disease, poverty, alienation that we as the Christian community may be present with them, and not merely offer them our good intentions, let us pray to the Lord.

Celebrant:
Let your Holy Spirit, God, the Spirit of Jesus, come upon us, stir us, animate us to a life that struggles for the common good of all men. Through Christ our Lord.

Celebrant:
May the fire of the Lord our God burn forever in the love of N., and N.,.
For it is truly known that the Lord's love is made manifest in the flesh of
man and wife. As they walk, he walks with them, and as they live, he
lives too.

Leader:
As Christ loves his bride, the Church, may this man love and experience
his wife, let us pray to the Lord.

2.
As the Church loves Christ her Lord, may this woman love and be devoted
to her husband, let us pray to the Lord.

3.
That all things upon this earth become alive with the love of Christ, let us
pray to the Lord.

4.
For all words between man and wife, that they may be spoken out of the
heart of love, let us pray to the Lord.

5.
As the universe is a source of rejoicing to our Father, let N., and N., be a
constant source of joy to each other, let us pray to the Lord.

Celebrant:
May their love and goodness grow in splendor each day of their lives. May
the nearness of one to the other remind them always of the oneness of God
and man. Let their thoughts be gentle, and their touch be gentle, and the
night always be a comfort to them. And one morning, let all the governments of the world grow gentle, so their children may have reason to sing.

MARRIAGE

Celebrant:
For all the human family, and especially for *N.*, and *N.*, let us appeal
to God, that he who has gathered us in his Spirit may hear us through
his Son.

Leader:
For the family of man, that all may know the Father's love and by his
grace may answer it in deeds of love and sharing, let us pray to the Lord.

2.
For the Church, the bride of Christ, that unshaken faithfulness will move
mountains of indifference and apathy, kindling hope where is only despair,
let us pray to the Lord.

3.
For *N.* and *N.*, here joined in promises of love and mutual care, that
their union may enable both of them and each of them to enjoy life's
pleasures fully and to help create a better world, let us pray to the Lord.

4.
For any children *N.* and *N.* have, that they may draw the sustenance of
happy and productive lives from harmony and love in their parents, let
us pray to the Lord.

5.
For the universe which is sacred to our Father, since he created it out
of the love of his heart, let us pray to the Lord.

Celebrant:
Our father, whose love for us is pattern for the human covenant which
we here celebrate, grant to this new creation, this marriage of two persons,
the grace of mutual care and gift of self both toward each other and
toward you. Through Christ our Lord.

FUNERAL

Celebrant:
Join with me now in common prayer, in community intercession, for
N., for all the dead, and for the living human family left here to work,
to build, to create a witness to God.

Leader:
For the world and all its dead and dying, that fulfillment, light and peace
may be the common lot of all God's children, let us pray to the Lord.

2.
For the Church, for our pope, and our bishop, and for all pastors, that
our witness to man's purpose and his destiny may be a warm, bright
beacon in the world, let us pray to the Lord.

3.
For our sister (brother) *N.,* that she (he) who knew creative labor, joy
and suffering here may share Christ's risen life and happiness, let us
pray to the Lord.

4.
For the relatives and friends who suffer this loss, this pain of separation,
that our common faith and hope and love may be a strong support for
them, let us pray to the Lord.

5.
For all who are in agony of mind or body, that by our ministry, our
friendship and our help God's love may be made real to them, let us
pray to the Lord.

Celebrant:
Because your Son by dying has destroyed our death and by being raised
up has given us new life, hear these intercessions, our Father, and lift us
by your Spirit out of our shadows of uncertainty to the light of your
hope. Through Christ our Lord.

FUNERAL

Celebrant:
We who stand here in life cannot truly see the living God; we who pray here in life cannot truly know his living presence as our brother (sister) N., now knows him.

Leader:
The Lord our God shall not lose whom he has loved. That whoever has loved the Lord his God shall not lose him though he be torn from the hands of the living, though he travel past the rim of life, let us pray to the Lord.

2.
That death shall hold no terror for man and his dreams upon this earth, let us pray to the Lord.

3.
As Hiroshima has risen from the ashes, our brother (sister) N., shall rise to his (her) God, we pray to the Lord.

4.
As Christ suffered and died, so shall we, and so shall all we love. And as Christ rose to oneness divine, so shall we, and so shall all we love, we pray to the Lord.

5.
Though death is as intrinsic as rock upon this earth, so is the joy of the resurrection of man, we pray to the Lord.

Celebrant:
Lord, in our moment of suffering help us to remember our brothers and sisters who suffer now under poverty, oppression and war. Help us to comfort ourselves by comforting them. Help us to see the image of our brother (sister) N., living within them.

FUNERAL

Celebrant:
Thank God we can approach him in faith!
Without faith, without him, our hearts would be
too heavy to bear. In faith, let us pray.

Leader:
That as *(name)* crosses the threshold of death
to begin everlasting life, Jesus may be his/her
guide and companion, we pray.

2.
That the presence of friends and relatives in these days
may testify to God's constant presence and love, we pray.

3.
That the numbness in our hearts
may once again allow us to feel
pain and suffering, joy and laughter,
we pray.

4.
That the emptiness of our lives
may gradually be filled by the love
we know from others, from Christ, we pray.

5.
That the quiet flower of Jesus' triumphant life
may take root in our hearts through life and death,
we pray.

Celebrant:
Father, we thank you for your love and support.
Receive your servant *(name)* with love and kindness;
strengthen us in faith and hope through Christ
our Lord.

FUNERAL

Celebrant:
We believe that Jesus died and rose again;
and so it will be for those who died believing in him.
God will bring them into company with him.
With confidence, then, we offer our prayers.

Leader:
That our brother/sister *(name)* may receive the reward
promised those who keep your word,
we pray to the Lord.

2.
That the power of the resurrection
may transform mortality into unending life,
we pray to the Lord.

3.
That he/she may share with your saints
the joy, light, and peace of your presence in glory,
we pray to the Lord.

4.
That we who mourn
may know the consolation of your love,
we pray to the Lord.

5.
That strengthened by faith in your promise,
we may live toward the day of reunion in heaven,
we pray to the Lord.

Celebrant:
Father, God of all consolation,
you have sent light into darkness
in the presence and power of your Son.
His death and resurrection have given us
the victory over death itself.
Hear the prayers we offer for our brother/sister
in Christ who is our hope.

FUNERAL

Celebrant:

My sisters and brothers: we have gone down into the waters of baptism to be buried with Christ. In the shadow of this death which now clouds our joy, let us call upon the Father that he might lift us up to new life in the same Christ, our risen Lord.

Leader:

That we might find in the gift of tears
a tribute to the love the Father has shown us
in the life of *(name),* let us pray.

2.

That the life, love, and accomplishments of *(name)*
might be sustained by our acknowledgement
of all that she (he) has done
to bring us a sign of the Lord's abiding presence,
let us pray.

3.

That the faults and offences of *(name)*'s life
might stand in mute testimony to the Father's forgiveness of sins,
let us pray.

4.

That this passing over to new life
might move us to unite with all those
whose life and death is an experience of hunger,
injustice, and the ravages of war, let us pray.

5.

That all those who minister to the dying
might find the hearts and hands to help them
in their work, let us pray.

Celebrant:

God our Father, we never cease to thank you
for the new life which comes from your creative hands.

In our tears we beg you to fill the emptiness which attacks us in the face of death. Fill us again with your life-giving Spirit that with one voice we might profess our belief that the life you give us here is but the beginning of life with you forever. Hear this prayer in the name of our death-conquering Lord, Jesus Christ, your Son.

FUNERAL

Celebrant:
Jesus who died for us
shares with us his risen life.
Let us pray that we always be ready
to answer his call to new life.

Leader:
For the Church:
that we grow in our faith
in Jesus' power over death, we pray.

2.
For those of us who were close to *(name)*:
that the hope of new life in Jesus
may be our consolation and strength, we pray.

3.
For everyone here:
that the bread of heaven which we share
may be our food for everlasting life, we pray.

5.
For the whole world:
that the sadness caused by death
may be overcome by the presence
of the love of God,
in himself and in his Church, we pray.

Celebrant:
Father, we thank you for calling us
to believe in you, here on earth.
May we thank you when you call us forward
to live with you in heaven,
through Christ our Lord.

FUNERAL OF A MEMBER OF THE ARMED FORCES

Celebrant:
Let us ask our Father, who has seen his sons and daughters kill each other's dream, to take pity on us, to weep for us and give *(N.)* the new life of Jesus.

Leader:
For *(N.)* whom we sent to war, and for all the men we sent to die, that they will live on in us to remind us of the emptiness of hate, to remind us of the peace we cannot seem to attain, let us pray to the Lord.

2.
For *(N.)*'s family and all the families shattered by war, that they can find in their community the healing strength of your love, let us pray to the Lord.

3.
For *(N.)*'s friends and for everybody whose love has been killed in battle, that they will have the courage to continue giving the warmth of their hearts to those who are still alive, let us pray to the Lord.

4.
For the veterans who have returned from World War I, World War II, Korea, Vietnam and Cambodia, and all war veterans of the world, that their memory of the act of war will be barren and their anger at war's carnage will not stop until the world knows peace, let us pray to the Lord.

5.
For those mutilated by war in their hearts and bodies, that they will find hope in him who created them whole, and support from us, our brother's keeper, let us pray to the Lord.

Celebrant:
Father, grant to your son *(N.)*, now with you, peace and everlasting life; help us bear our loss and give us strength to pursue our quest for the unity and harmony of all men, through Christ, our Lord.